Anthropology
& Education gy available to educators and
their students. It is hoped and
believed, however, that it will also prove valuable to those in other
professions and in the several disciplines that comprise the behavioral sciences.

In recent years some educators have discovered that anthropology has much to offer the areas of professional training and educational theory and practice. In its cross-cultural comparisons of human behavior and in its inductive, empirical method of analysis are
found a conceptual freshness that is intellectually liberating.

Actually, there are four major areas of anthropological theory
which have direct relevance for education. These are the transmission of culture and learning processes; the regularities of behavior
and belief which we call culture; the ways in which individuals
group themselves for the accomplishment of communal purposes,
from which comes organization theory; and the processes by which
transformations occur in human behavior and groupings which can
be explained by a theory of change. In addition, there are the subject-matter areas of child rearing; community and the relationships
among institutions within it; the rites of passage; the cultural categories of social class, ethnic group, age, grading, and sex; and others.

These several areas of theory and substance provide a rich
source for this series. For example, there are plans for analyses of
the relevance of anthropology to each educational specialty, such as
administration, guidance, and curriculum. In another direction, the
perspective and method of such areas as social anthropology, applied anthropology, and linguistics in relation to education will be
examined. Several studies about educational activities which use
anthropological research methods and concepts will appear. Other
subject areas for the series include the culture of childhood, comparative educational systems, methods of research, and the exempli-
fication of anthropological theory in subject-matter organization. It
is believed that the availability of such a storehouse of knowledge
in the several volumes in this series will contribute immensely to the
further improvement of our educational system.

Solon T. Kimball, *General Editor*

THE
CULTURE
OF
CHILDHOOD

**Child's-Eye Views of
Society and Culture**

MARY ELLEN GOODMAN

Teachers College Press
Teachers College, Columbia University

The excerpts from *Children of Crisis* by Robert Coles are reprinted by permission of Atlantic - Little, Brown and Co. Copyright© 1964, 1965, 1966, 1967 by Robert Coles.

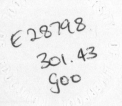
Manufactured in the United States of America

*This book is dedicated to
the late
Gordon W. Allport, whose
sane, sensitive, and humane
psychology has inspired
and illuminated all my
efforts in cultural anthropology*

Great changes in the destiny of
mankind can be effected only in
the minds of little children.

Herbert Read

Contents

Foreword

It is a particular pleasure for me to write this foreword to Mary Ellen Goodman's new book, mixed with deep sorrow that she did not live to see its publication. I knew her and admired her work for a number of years. When she was still a student at Harvard with our mutual friend, the late distinguished psychologist Gordon Allport (to whom she dedicated this volume), she visited me at Columbia and we talked a little about the research she was then conducting. I could only react with an enthusiasm that turned out to be entirely justified, since this work of hers led to the publication of *Race Awareness in Young Children*, a classic investigation that has been frequently cited and that played a part in the Supreme Court's desegregation decision in 1954. Although her principal disciplinary identification was with cultural anthropology, she also remained faithful to her early psychological training, and the present volume is eloquent testimony to her ability to look at problems of "culture and personality" in truly interdisciplinary terms.

The culture of childhood—the manner in which children in different societies see themselves and are seen by adults, the values and attitudes that children take from others or discover for themselves—has been touched on in many anthropological monographs and has been the subject of a considerable amount of sociological and psychological research. The literature on the subject is rich, but scattered and localized. This volume gives us an overview of its content and variety, but, more important, it orders and integrates the material into a coherent unity. The children described come from a wide range of cultures—the Philippines, Java, Puerto Rico, New Zealand (the Maori), Japan (her own research), Mexico, China, and Egypt, and in the United States include the Amish, the Negroes, and "ordinary" Americans. The subjects treated also range widely, including the training of children, the patterns of politeness, occupational preferences, play, language habits, peer cultures, and many others. Even so, the sophisticated reader may feel that some problems and places have been rather neglected; all I can say is that what is included is definitely worth reading.

I believe also that this book should perform the added function of stimulating further research on the culture of children. The author raises a number of issues in connection with which she herself indicates that the data are as yet inadequate. Sometimes the breakdowns in her tables leave very few cases in an individual cell, and this should encourage replication studies of larger samples. Her own demonstration of the manner in which qualitative (ethnological) observations may be supplemented by quantitative (usually psychological) data should encourage others to attempt a similar integration.

This book, small in size but rich in content, is a welcome addition to our growing knowledge of the intimate and intricate relation between culture and the development of personality.

Otto Klineberg

November, 1969

Postscript

I talked briefly with Mary Ellen Goodman about *The Culture of Childhood* in November, 1968. We were both in Seattle at the annual meeting of the American Anthropological Association, where she had come with her daughter, who had commenced graduate studies in anthropology. A few weeks later she sent me the final revision of her manuscript for review and forwarding to the publishers.

Shortly afterwards I learned the sad news that she had died. I had been informed earlier that she had been seriously ill and that it had been a painful struggle for her to muster the energy to bring the manuscript to its completion.

Mary Ellen Goodman was uniquely qualified to write this book. Her professional career had been devoted to the study of children. I have no doubt but that future research and thinking about early childhood development and learning will be influenced by her writings. She was an intelligent, dedicated, and charming individual and the educational world is in her debt for this final gift.

Solon Kimball

January, 1970

Introduction

Singularly little systematic attention has been given to the child's perception of parental behavior—or, for that matter, to the child's perception of anything.

Robert and Elizabeth Dubin

The American way of life has been characterized, and caricatured too, as child-centered to an extreme degree. Visitors from abroad have been known to observe that the vaunted American democracy is in fact a pedocracy, and that the most surprising fact of American life is the way parents obey their children. Many of us might wish to argue these conclusions, but few of us could object to the statement that Americans generally are intensely concerned about the welfare of their children, and anxious lest they be provided with less than "the best" in education, health care, and optimum conditions for full development of personality and personal potential.

Anthropologists, whose business it is to study and compare the lifeways—the cultures—of peoples through time and around the globe, find the focus on childhood in American culture unique. We have set a new record; no other people seems ever to have been so preoccupied with children, so anxious about them, or so uncertain of how to deal with them.

In view of this it is astonishing that our researchers have devoted so little attention to the "culture of childhood." References to "middle-class culture" are commonplace, and "the culture of poverty" has become a focus of research attention and general concern. Ethnic and religious minorities turn up in most of the large and complex societies, and each minority practices a way of life which is in some degree distinctive. Most of these kinds of subcultures are

1

well known; most of them have been studied in some depth. But the very concept, "culture of childhood," is rarely mentioned. It was only long after I had begun to think and talk about the culture of childhood that I discovered one or two other researchers who, independently, had coined the same phrase. I find myself still one of a very small company of scholars for whom the culture of childhood has long been a major research focus. Careful searching through the literature in psychology and sociology, as well as in anthropology, has proved this point. Therefore, because of the scarcity of such studies and due to my personal taste for the fruits of my own labors in the academic vineyard, data from my own research may seem conspicuous in this book.

The literature on child development, including a scholarly journal published under that name, is enormous. So is the literature on child rearing—on socialization. These and other studies report what adults see when they observe children, and what adults do for and to children. Culture of childhood studies, in contrast, report on what children see as they observe the world in which they find themselves. Because culture of childhood studies are few I have found it necessary to supplement them to some extent by drawing inferences about the "child's-eye view" from child development or from socialization studies. However, this has been done sparingly and with caution.

American cults, systems, and theories of pedagogy and of child rearing are constructed upon knowledge and assumptions about children—their capacities, interests, and inclinations at various ages and stages. Assumptions must do where knowledge is either inadequate or ignored, but the systems built upon them are likely to be faulty at best, and disastrous at worst. Modern American practices in child rearing have been judged to be, on average, less than satisfactory. Certain pedagogical practices of ours have been severely criticized. Shortcomings in both child rearing and pedagogy are, in part, attributable to fallacious assumptions about the culture of childhood.

In this book I have brought together a large part of the all too scanty data illuminating that culture. These data should help to correct at least two of the fallacious assumptions underlying much of American pedagogy and child rearing: (1) the fallacy of universal age/stage linkages, and (2) the underestimation fallacy.

A conspicuous and highly mischievous instance of the former is the assumption that adolescence is necessarily a period of storm and stress. That strangely tenacious myth should, as a result of anthropologists' findings, have long ago been laid to rest. These findings show clearly that adolescents behave and work like mature men and women in many societies. In other societies they play; the boys "sow wild oats" and the girls enjoy a period of such idle dalliance as they have not known before and will not know again. What makes the difference? It is clearly a matter of differences in culturally patterned expectations, in training, and in social controls. Adolescence as an age—a developmental phase—does not determine the behavior of adolescents; child rearing and other aspects of the cultural patterning may.

Among Americans the underestimation fallacy flourishes and undermines the intuitive insights of wise parents and teachers. The problem is the inability of many adults to appreciate the extent of a child's perceptions, his ability to understand interpersonal relations, and his ability to cope with frustrations, tensions, and troubles. It is true that his perceptions, understandings, and his ability to handle his emotions and problems are likely to differ both qualitatively and quantitatively from those of the adult. The child's lesser ability to verbalize will of itself reduce the fullness and clarity of his communications, if not of his conceptualizations. But the differences are of degree, not of kind.

In what follows I hope to substantiate these views. One reservation must be added, however, and kept always in mind: there are, in any society, individual differences that assert themselves in spite of cultural pull or press. The occasional deviants—"odd balls," geniuses, morons, or rebels—are universals in human experience. Here we shall not attempt to explore the complex interplay of genetic givens with features of developmental context. Whatever the specifics of this interplay, individuality is never completely obliterated. However, it is equally true that individuals vary, apparently from birth, in their readiness to respond to context. They vary also with respect to forcefulness of individual thrust, of assertiveness, and of innovative inclination. Cultures vary in their tightness or looseness—in the extent to which they exert press and pull or invite and reward individual thrust. This important matter is treated more extensively in another book of mine, *The Individual and Culture*.

What the child knows and what parts of the total culture he commands will, of course, vary with a number of factors. His age, sex, intelligence, curiosity, insight, and amount of both formal and informal education will combine to affect the extent of his knowledge. The social class and ethnic positions of his parents, and of other people who make up the child's social world, will, to some extent, affect his opportunities to develop a cultural repertoire. They may affect also his motivations to do so.

3

It must be remembered too that the child's knowledge will reflect the nature and complexity of the total society and culture in which he finds himself. Small folkish societies bearing nonliterate cultures present to children a comparatively narrow range of possibilities and alternatives. In large urban-industrial societies bearing sophisticated and complex cultures the range is wide. However, in either case, the culture of childhood, measured against the context, is likely to prove impressive.

Here we are concerned with child's-eye views of the world, rather than with enculturation—the processes through which those views are acquired. But these basic facts must be noted:

However folkish or sophisticated the culture, much enculturation goes on at levels not properly described as conscious, explicit, or formal. Much teaching, learning, and cultural transmission, especially in the realm of beliefs, ideas and ideals, is subconscious, implicit, or informal. Adult expectations are transmitted mainly casually or in subtle ways. . . . The realm of the conscious, explicit, and formal in enculturation expands greatly with increasing cultural complexity. Where the on-coming generation must learn much that is abstract and esoteric (the highly specialized knowledge of the physician or lawyer, for example), enculturation can no longer be left to chance and to the adults of the child's personal community. The whole vast structure of formal education in contemporary urban-industrial societies rests on this elementary fact and its inherent logic.

What is commonly taught and learned during childhood in non-literate cultures is
—knowledge, attitudes, and practices designed to protect the child from injury and illness, natural and supernatural;
—knowledge, skills, habits, and attitudes necessary if the child is to become an adult capable of coping with the environment and meeting the conditions for survival and necessary assistance to dependents;
—knowledge, attitudes, values, and practices intended to transform the ignorant and willful child into a "good citizen"—a person of admired character type—who has the admired qualities, who understands and respects others' rights, and who maintains the proprieties (in toilet habits and sex behavior, for example).[1]

In what follows we examine basics of the culture of childhood from infancy into adolescence. Our cross-cultural method of examination enables us to both identify and compare similarities and differences. Premature conclusions concerning universals, some of them resting on parochial or ethnocentric views, are widely current. There has been too much inclination to assume that what seems to be true of childhood in American or in other Western societies is necessarily true of childhood universally. We are in need of the perspective, and the correctives, that the comparative anthropological view alone provides.

[1]Mary Ellen Goodman, *The Individual and Culture* (Homewood, Ill.: The Dorsey Press, 1967), p. 133.

1

Infancy and Early Childhood: Attention, Patterns, and Learning

Pattern, relative to other stimulus variables, has high attention value for young
infants.

Robert L. Fantz

The culture of childhood, like all cultures, is learned, shared, and transmitted. It is to some degree learned by children from one another. Mainly, however, it is learned from adults. It is learned, but not necessarily taught. There is reason to believe that two phenomena lie at the heart of this learning process—attention and patterns.

Anthropologists' reports are full of evidence that children everywhere pay keen attention to the world around them. It is in the nature of children to be intensely curious about that world and eager to play a part in it. Accumulating evidence indicates that their awareness of what goes on around them is greater by far, and manifested earlier, than is recognized by most Americans who consider themselves knowledgeable about children.

Each child is born into a society whose members practice a way of life—a culture. The basis for the continued existence of a society and its culture is orderliness. Individual deviations and variations notwithstanding, there are prevailing patterns of organization and behavior, some of which are perceptible even to very young infants. Mother and other principal household figures come and go through the child's field of vision; food and other interesting objects are brought into or carried through his field of vision; daylight and darkness come and go. These and other dynamisms of the child's world will be to some extent variable, even erratic, but he will show a remarkable capacity for isolating regularities—patterned features —from what is not patterned.

Infants learn rapidly to recognize a wide variety of the patterns to which they are repeatedly exposed and to which they pay attention. Each face that comes often before the child constitutes a physical pattern, a unique configuration that becomes rapidly familiar. Each repeated sequence or event comes to be recognized as a whole, as a patterned progression. The appearance of the mother or a mother surrogate, for example; the appearance of her breast or some other food source; the grasping of that source and taking from it is an obvious and universal patterned progression.

The child's attentiveness, his interest in this and many other kinds of patterns, are not merely expressions of his needs for human response, for food, or for other essential satisfactions. Such needs are certainly universal and universally relevant to the process of pattern perception. But now we have evidence of a most interesting, important, and long-overlooked fact about attentiveness and pattern perception: sensitivity to surroundings is at a maximum when the infant is relaxed and satisfied; hunger or other tensions are not essential to high levels of perception. It is in the nature of the human organism to be intellectually active.

Attentive Behavior and Pattern Discrimination in Infancy

The earliness and nature of attentive behavior and pattern discrimination have been dramatically demonstrated. Studies of infants less than two weeks old (seven of them less than twenty-four hours old!) have shown that they can and do pay selective attention to patterns (stripes, for example).

This shows that the eye and brain are sufficiently well developed at birth to provide the basic visual capacities necessary to form perception. And since the highest level in the visual system, the striate cortex, is necessary for pattern vision, it may be concluded that the new-born infant is not entirely restricted to a subcortical level of brain function, as often assumed.[1]

The high attention value of pattern relative to other stimulus variables . . . is in opposition to the traditional belief that color, brightness, and size are primary sense qualities, whereas form perception is secondary and acquired. . . . The individual is able to walk or crawl without bumping into

8

things or falling off edges largely because he notices variations in surface patterning or contouring which indicate an obstacle or a dropoff in the path ahead . . . [He is] able to recognize objects . . . [including] people . . . In particular, the configuration of the face and head is the best means of distinguishing a human being. . . .[2]

. . . This early perceptual contact (rather than either physical contact or need reduction) may be the primary basis for the development of sociability in humans.[3]

The world of the infant is patterned and organized. This world is selectively explored in the only way possible for the helpless but visually active infant.[4]

It has been shown too, in contradiction to long-standing assumptions, that infants give maximum attentiveness to the world around them when they are physically relaxed and free of visceral tensions or discomforts. It is not body needs for "tension reduction" that drive the organism; rather, the mainspring is intellectual, a matter of curiosity and interests. Moreover, "meaningful encounters with the environment are . . . at least one of the critical factors which maintains the state of alertness, even during [early] infancy."[5] Interest begets exploration, which begets further interest.

At least three researchers (Robert L. Fantz, Peter H. Wolff, and Bettye M. Caldwell) agree that an important element of "meaningful encounter" is novelty. Caldwell says: "Whatever else familiarity might breed, it seems almost certain to lead to a diminution of interest." She finds, for example, that babies of three months or more, observed when both their mothers and a stranger are present, look "significantly more" at the stranger.[6] Curiosity and an appreciation of novelty are powerful factors in connection with attention and learning, and they are in the nature of man from birth.

Culturally Patterned Expectations and Attention-Focusing

Attentiveness and learning are fostered by culture as well as by inherent inclinations. In each culture there are patterned (customary) ideas and expectations about the nature, capacities, and proper behavior of children. These patterns may have some foundation in the biological givens; for example, the American expectation that boys will be stronger, rougher, more aggressive and active than girls. On average, and quite naturally, they are; nature has sex-linked these attributes. However, the expectation very soon gets communicated to children of both sexes. Both respond obligingly by

9

behaving more or less in accord with what they understand to be the ways appropriate to their sex. Natural inclinations are thereby strengthened, even exaggerated. But the patterned expectations may deviate from the natural tendencies, and still the average child will strive to meet those expectations. In some societies boys at the tender age of four are expected never to cry or to shed tears. Where there are sanctioned patterns of premarital chastity we have even more impressive evidence of cultural patterning noncongruent with "what comes naturally."

Still other patterns have little to do, one way or another, with natural endowments or inclinations. They represent ideals, beliefs about what children *ought* to be, rather than about what they inherently *are*. The list of "oughts" set forth by Filipino mothers in a recent study is by no means unusual; parents in many traditional (pre-urban/industrial) societies would find in it little with which to disagree.

. . . Docility, subordination to elders, . . . respect for the wisdom of older people, gratitude to parents for having been born, and a recognition of the greater good of the family as a whole. . . .

The individual avoids overt conflict; he makes his parents happy by his cheerfulness; and he shows a pattern of personal pride. Above all, parents want their children to have good dispositions.[7]

One expectation commonly expressed by American parents that is missing from this Filipino roster is "the hope that their children will be ambitious or show great achievements. There is no mention of a child becoming rich or famous."[8] The expectations of American parents traditionally, and of many today, are in sharp contrast. Stress on ambition and industriousness are characteristic of the upwardly mobile segments of complex urban-industrial societies and of the more "modernized" segments of "developing" societies.

Cultural patterning affecting the culture of childhood takes the form not only of expectations but of role definitions—descriptions of and directions for proper behavior.

Role definitions change with age, particularly over the years up to adulthood. With the changes . . . the child's behavior also changes.

Behavior modifications can be abrupt and dramatic as in the case of those societies in which *rites de passage* [for example, ceremonies marking societal coming-of-age] are observed, or they can show a slower rate of change with wider individual differences. Children can go from dependence to independence, albeit painfully, if a society so defines an expected role

10

shift. Aggression can be expressed up to a certain age and then sharply curtailed.[9]

[In each culture] the transition from one stage to another is determined by the society's . . . concept of [the child's] . . . mental capacities at a given time.[10]

Concepts concerning the capacities of children—mental capacities and other kinds as well—are as much part of the cultural patterning as are role definitions for children.

In many, perhaps in most societies, infants and small children are thought of primarily in terms of incapacities and inabilities. They are thought of in such terms as "senseless," unable to reason, unaware, fragile, susceptible, unable to respond to teaching or direction. In view of these ideas it is not surprising that they are usually treated with a kind of amiable tolerance; little is expected of them in the way of learning, control, or responsibility.

Culturally patterned opinions about rates of maturation, whether and how they can be altered, and about individual differences vary widely. In some societies (the Philippines, for example),[11] it is believed that maturation is slow (children don't begin to have "sense" until four or later), that it can't be hurried, and that it is a highly individualistic matter. In other societies (in Khalapur, India, for example),[12] there is no particular concern with maturation, and certainly none with stimulating or motivating the child to learn. Young children are thought of as passive and much like one another, as requiring mainly protection and essential physical care.

A third variant in the range of patterned ideas about infancy and early childhood puts emphasis on speedy training for work and responsibility (among the Gusii of Kenya, for example).[13] Once the infant is weaned, at about age two, he is considered capable of being trained; rapidly, and with considerable severity, he is forced into obedience and the assumption (by age six or seven) of near-adult responsibilities. Earlier but less severe teaching and training are customary in some societies (the Jicarilla Apache Indians, for example).[14] The Apache say: "When the baby is about a year old we begin to teach it."[15] Verbal instruction is generously employed. Clearly the Apache regard one-year-olds as quite capable of responding to teaching and training. At about this time ". . . parents and close relatives, particularly those of the maternal line, initiate a persistent process of training and correction."[16]

The patterns peculiar to the American "tribe"—to contemporary middle-class New Englanders, at any rate—illustrate still another variant. The people of "Orchard Town, U.S.A.," think of the child as a bundle of potentialities to be realized. However, their own responsibilities in sustaining and enhancing, while not arresting the developmental process, weigh heavily upon them. They are anxious lest they fail to read correctly what they believe to be highly individualized signs of readiness, of responsiveness. Parents, pediatricians, and later teachers as well, scrutinize each child for reassurance that he is receiving proper care and guidance. They watch for clues to his needs, which are believed to emerge and change through natural stages of development. Solicitous attention is accompanied by minimal expectations with respect to assumption by the child of work or other types of responsibilities.[17]

These, then, are some of the many forces that underlie attention-focusing by children and create conditions that affect the learning of a culture of childhood: (1) such inherent capacities and inclinations as curiosity and interest in patterns and in novelties; (2) such culturally patterned pressures and incentives as expectations, ideals, role prescriptions, and ideas about the abilities and capacities of infants and young children. This is no doubt an incomplete listing of the basic and relevant forces. However, it will serve at least to illustrate a principle essential to our considerations here.

The principle is that in all societies nature and nurture conspire together to propel children, and usually to propel them rapidly, toward command of significant portions of the cultures borne by their societies. The child has really no choice; his cultural learnings will be limited only by his inherent intellectual capacities and his cultural exposures. Cultural exposures vary widely as a function of the nature and complexity of the total culture; for example, no child can learn to read in a nonliterate culture. They vary too as a function of opportunities to observe and to participate; for example, no child can develop early a realistic concept of death if he has neither observed it, even at the subhuman level, nor participated in efforts to prevent it, nor in the "grief business" that follows it.

NOTES

[1] Robert L. Fantz, "Visual Perception from Birth as Shown by Pattern Selectivity," *Annals of the New York Academy of Sciences*, 118 (1965), 799.

[2] *Ibid.*, pp. 805 f.

[3] *Ibid.*, p. 809.

[4] *Ibid.*, p. 812.

[5] Peter H. Wolff, "The Development of Attention in Young Infants," *Annals of the New York Academy of Sciences*, 118 (1965), 822.

[6] Bettye M. Caldwell, "Discussion of Papers by Fantz, Wolff and Greenberg," *ibid.*, 861.

[7] George M. Guthrie and Pepita Jiminez Jacobs, *Child Rearing and Personality Development in the Philippines* (University Park and London: The Pennsylvania State University Press, 1966), p. 180.

[8] *Ibid.*, pp. 180 f.

[9] *Ibid.*, p. 9 (italics original).

[10] *Ibid.*, p. 23.

[11] William Nydegger and Corinne Nydegger, "Tarong: An Ilocos Barrio in the Philippines," in Beatrice B. Whiting, ed., *Six Cultures* (New York: John Wiley & Sons, 1963).

[12] Leigh Minturn and John T. Hitchcock, "The Rajputs of Khalapur, India," in Whiting, *op. cit.*

[13] Robert A. Le Vine and Barbara B. Le Vine, "Nyansongo: A Gusu Community in Kenya," in Whiting, *op. cit.*

[14] Morris E. Opler, *Childhood and Youth in Jicarilla Apache Society* (Los Angeles: The Southwest Museum, 1946).

[15] *Ibid.*, p. 25.

[16] *Ibid.*, p. 38.

[17] John L. Fischer and Ann Fischer, "The New Englanders of Orchard Town, U.S.A.," in Whiting, *op. cit.*

2

Infancy and Early Childhood: Language and Understandings

... The individual discovers the characteristics of reality as he goes along; ...
language ... plays an intimate part in this
discovery....

Joseph Church

"A child is born a speaker and born into a world of speakers."[1] It is in the nature of children to learn language, along with other fundamentals of a culture. All babies (with extremely rare exceptions in the cases of isolated children) are exposed to language from birth. All normal children learn the language, or the languages, to which they are exposed, and they do so as naturally and as inevitably as they learn to walk. Command of a significant part of the language of his people is an essential part, perhaps *the* essential part, of the child's culture.

What the child first hears must be a "big blooming buzzing confusion," just as an exotic language is to an adult. The child's rapid analysis of the fundamental units of his parents' language is one of the most astonishing facts in his career, and we are far from understanding how it occurs.[2]

In the case of the child, as in the case of the adult confronted with an exotic language, command usually lags behind comprehension. It is believed by some experts that children first hear and discriminate between consonants and vowels, next between types of consonants, and so on toward finer and finer discriminations and combinations. This theory is not proved, though there is supporting evidence.[3] However, to hear and discriminate between phonemes

15

(minimal sound units in a language) is not necessarily to be able to reproduce them.

Babies from nine months may begin to produce language to a limited extent. It is difficult to identify these beginnings; real words may be embedded in a "stream of expressive jargon" or they may function as "one-word sentences."[4] Very soon the jargon is likely to disappear "and the child settles down to speaking in one-word utterances—interjections, denomination (naming) and commands especially."[5]

It has been said that the child's initial vocabulary consists of nouns, since objects are the first things to have names. Nouns do predominate in the speech of young children, but the child is perfectly capable of using verbs, adjectives, and adverbs referring to meaningful aspects of his experience.[6]

Language in the Culture of Childhood

What American psychologists know about the language of young children is based almost entirely on studies made in this country or in related European language communities. Few anthropologists have studied child language intensively. However, available scraps of information suggest wide variation in the language of childhood as in other aspects of child culture. For example; where tonal pitch is an essential part of the patterning of language, children can and do produce it early.

In Chinese, as in many languages, pitch contrasts distinguish words. Chao (1951) reported that his grandchild learned tone contrasts very early, and, in stressed syllables, her system was almost the same as Standard Mandarin by twenty-eight months.[7]

Children learn very early not only how to speak a language, but also how to select linguistic formulae to fit the occasion and the relationships between speaker and persons spoken to. Modern American usage is peculiarly unselective in these matters; many American children no longer are expected to speak "respectfully" or "politely" to their elders, to strangers, or to authorities. Once the expectation dropped out of the cultural patterning among adults, it dropped rapidly out of the child culture as well. There are American educators and other "experts" who assume that young children are not able to meet such expectations. The assumption no doubt reflects ignorance of the fact that around the world there are cultures of childhood in which linguistic and gestural respect usages loom large indeed. From

16

Java comes but one of the many illustrations that might be advanced:

> . . . the child learns to communicate with his mother in the same familiar form that she uses to him, but from the beginning of his attempts to talk there is a deliberate attempt to make him use the polite phrases to all others. Thus, a child's first recognizable word is often *njuwun*, "I humbly beg for it;" and I have often seen children little more than a year old, barely able to stand, go through a polite bow and say an approximation of the high word for good-bye (only approximately correct phonetically but with accurate intonation, intonation being all important in polite contexts). . . . Politeness learning is highly emphasized by the *prijaji* (people of aristocratic value orientation), and a *prijaji* child of five or six already has an extensive repertoire of graceful phrases and actions.[8]

Speed of language learning is affected by the extent to which cultural press (via adult urging) and cultural pull (via rewards and recognitions) are exerted. Among the world's peoples many have developed such patternings. Arapaho Indians (now of Wyoming and Oklahoma) believed that the meadow larks and the crows spoke their language. Little children customarily were fed the cooked meat and eggs of the lark (not the crow, however); "the belief was that a child so fed would talk early and have knowledge of things. . . . Moving the meadow lark's bill back and forth between the child's lips was also thought to make it talk." In earlier days a child's parents celebrated its first words by giving a feast for the old men and women of the tribe.[9] The Chippewa Indians (now of Wisconsin, Minnesota, and Michigan) urged and rewarded the learning of names of objects. An adult would hold up the object and repeat its name until the child correctly reproduced the sounds. Often he would give the object to the child.[10]

In his language learning, as in his learning of other aspects of a general culture, the child is limited mainly by the extent and nature of the language usage to which he is exposed. "Speech defects" or inadequacies do appear for other reasons too, but these unusual cases will not concern us here. Exposures vary especially with respect to (1) usage of baby talk; (2) syntax and vocabulary; and (3) mono- or bilingualism.

Is baby talk of some sort universally a feature of the culture of childhood? At least one expert believes that it is. Going even further, he argues that . . . "baby language is an international language. If we make a short list of the earliest words actually spoken by children, with their meanings, we have a vocabulary that every one will recognize."[11] But a later study convincingly refutes M. M. Lewis.

17

Charles A. Ferguson has compared baby talk in six languages from widely separated cultures, five of them linguistically unrelated (Syrian Arabic, Marathi, Comanche, Gilyak, English, and Spanish). His systematic comparison of words for thirty persons, things, and activities turns up remarkably few striking coincidences. Nearly all of the identities or close similarities appear in the two related languages (English and Spanish). Beyond those the only similarities are between the English *mommy*, Spanish *mama*, Arabic *māma*, Marathi *(m)ai*, and Gilyak *yma*.[12]

Ferguson refutes another widely held belief—that babies and young children invent baby talk. He shows that it is in fact learned by the young because their elders speak to them in this "language." The elders learned it in their time in the same way, and the children will in turn eventually transmit it to the next generation. Intergenerational transmission is one of the criteria for identifying items of behavior that are culturally patterned (culture is a vast collection of patterns that are learned, shared, and transmitted). Baby talk meets the test, except to the extent that it is specific to a particular family, either invented by the adults or by the children. Some few items of this unusual sort occur in every family; in our family "spaghetti" was for several years known as nothing but "besgetee," because we all elected to adopt this item from our son's linguistic idiosyncracies. Baby talk eventually changes as a result of the disuse of once standard items and the "catching on" of certain innovations. But its general persistence is remarkable. Ferguson reports:

. . . there is a record of Arabic baby talk used at the beginning of the nineteenth century which is very much like Arabic baby talk today. An even more impressive case is the persistence of baby talk words for food, drink, and sleep for some two thousand years in the Mediterranean area.[13]

Language in Subcultures

The syntax and vocabulary commanded by young children will in all societies represent a sizable fraction of what is commanded by the average adults of each society. In complex societies like our own certain adult subsocieties—the highly educated, the occupationally specialized—command a linguistic culture well above average in size and complexity. Conversely, there are "disadvantaged" or "deprived" social segments whose linguistic culture is comparatively limited. The language commanded by young children ordinarily reflects the level of command common in the social segment to which his parents and other members of his personal community belong.

From early infancy children respond to the presence and to the vocalizations of older persons. Recent controlled observations support this commonplace of casual observation. It has been shown that "the primary influence on infant babbling is the human voice . . . [and that] other stimuli, such as the presence of an adult, can enhance the voice's potential for increasing infant vocalizations."[14] Beyond this basic phenomenon the details of the uniquely human process of language learning, though much studied and argued by American and European psychologists, remain obscure. It is known, however, that mere "imitation, input storage, and practice" cannot alone account for language learning.[15] One expert tells us:

All children are able to understand and construct sentences they have never heard but which are nevertheless well-formed, well formed in terms of general rules that are implicit in the sentences the child has heard. Somehow, then, every child processes the speech to which he is exposed so as to induce from it a latent structure [the implicit general rules of the language] . . . The discovery of latent structure is the greatest of the processes involved in language learning and the most difficult to understand.[16]

However, the child's "discovery of latent structure" must be always relative. He seldom discovers what does not exist in his world of language usage. Where that world is impoverished, as compared with neighboring worlds, so too his extrapolations will be.

In this fact lies the source of linguistic limitations exhibited by lower-class children in large, class-differentiated societies. It is reported that the speech patterns of "working-class" English children by age five show "fewer and shorter dependent clauses, and fewer optional adverbial and nominal qualifiers and fewer negatives" than appear in children of the middle and upper class. These social class-associated patterns have been labeled "restricted code" (working class) and "elaborated code" (middle and upper class). "Restricted codes tend to be syntactically redundant, elliptical, narrative, concrete, with richer use of expressive vocal features."[17]

Studies in the United States support and confirm these findings by English sociologist Basil Bernstein. Lower-class children, and their mothers too, show "less abstraction and more simple relational responses."[18] There is evidence also that "divergences between classes increase with age. . . ."[19] Class and caste differences in linguistic culture are sometimes so great as to amount to different dialects.

. . . Negro-white dialect diversity in northern cities has increased in the past thirty years because of the development of very large enclaves in cities like

19

Detroit and New York City, reducing inter-group contacts (McDavid, 1951), and because of the development of anti-white values among younger Negroes (Labov, 1964).[20]

Children whose linguistic culture is confined to under-caste dialects or restricted codes are hampered with respect to command of other and related aspects of culture. In this country "widespread deficiencies ranging across the cognitive, affective, motivational, and social areas have been found in [culturally] deprived children. . . . *Their behavior reflects the lack of a symbolic system by which to organize the plentiful stimulation surrounding them* [when they are placed in situations—headstart programs, for example—offering compensatory enrichment].[21] Their "lack of a symbolic system" is in large part a linguistic lack. "Deprived preschool children do not have a firm language base for thinking. They will develop one only if they are given consistent guidance."[22]

Language and Thinking

The importance of the "language base for thinking" hardly can be overestimated. The relation between language and thought is not understood in detail, but its existence is undeniable.

For it must be remembered that language is learned not as an abstract system for representing and operating on the world, but in the process of so operating; it comes complete with subject matter, with content, so that in learning language the child simultaneously learns about the world and its properties, including innumerable moral and esthetic conventions.[23]

It is clear that self-control and self-direction vary directly with cognitive maturity, and especially with the ability to manipulate situations symbolically, to anticipate consequences, to weigh, to judge, and to decide between alternatives.[24]

The subtleties of interplay between a child's linguistic culture and his value orientations are illustrated by comparison of Puerto Rican and middle-class non-Puerto Rican children in New York. A study shows that the latter are much more oriented toward problem-solving and task-mastery, the former toward people—toward interpersonal relations. The researchers who conducted the study suggest that the basic difference resides in language and the prevailing uses of it.

The style of the [Puerto Rican] culture may be one in which verbalizations

20

are heavily weighted to communicate affective and social contents rather than task-directed ones, with the result that the ability to engage in verbal behavior in response to a cognitive demand fails to develop in the same way that it does in the middle-class children.[25]

These differences are clear cut in three-year-olds. Barring radical interventions they will persist and intensify. As children of the two groups attain school age and experience the educational system's verbalized demands for cognitive performance, their different orientations "can result only in a much enhanced likelihood for school failure and underachievement in the Puerto Rican children and for school success in the middle-class children."[26]

In the United States there has been a widespread notion that bilingualism in child culture is necessarily a handicap and undesirable. However, "multilingualism is the rule in many communities in the world, . . ." and the children of such communities (in Switzerland, for example) are not on average notably disadvantaged. On the contrary, "the child may have discernible intellectual advantages from his mastery of two languages and his greater conceptual flexibility. . ."[27]

Large numbers of American studies have purported to show otherwise. Nearly all of them are obviously fallacious, because they ignore all variables except bilingualism. The simple fact is that in this country nearly all children who are bilingual are also otherwise culturally differentiated from the average middle-class American child. Usually they are, as a result, at a disadvantage in American schools, and score low on the standard school tests (the Puerto Rican children discussed earlier are a case in point). And these bilinguals ordinarily belong not only to a culturally differentiated subsociety but also to one that is subordinated in relation to the dominant—the white/Anglo-Saxon/Protestant—majority. What is attributed to bilingualism is in fact the result of other and multiple handicaps to which children bearing non-majority cultures are exposed in American society. Currently and belatedly, this fact is being recognized, and studies that presume to show that "bilingualism of itself produced intellectual deficit are beyond the pale of responsible inquiry."[28]

Studies pointing out the advantages of bilingualism are few, recent, and convincing. One excellent study of this type concludes:

The picture that emerges of the French-English bilingual in Montreal is that of a youngster whose wider experiences in two cultures have given him advantages which a monolingual does not enjoy. Intellectually his experience with two language systems seems to have left him with a mental flexibility, a superiority in concept formation, and a more diversified set of mental abilities. . . . In contrast, the monolingual appears to have a more unitary structure of intelligence which he must use for all types of intellectual tasks.[29]

The handicap that some bilingual children exhibit should probably be attributed to their unfavorable social situation since others, who come from more advantageous surroundings, find bilingualism an asset.

The evidence permits us to conclude that the child speaks the language of his society as naturally and as inevitably as he walks. Language is an essential part, and perhaps *the* essential part, of a culture of childhood. In spite of wide variation between languages, as between other aspects of culture, children learn with apparent ease whatever may be the linguistic patterns of their culture (the tone contrasts of Chinese, for example). They learn with equal facility the verbal usages (such as terms of address) appropriate to particular persons and situations. Speed of language learning is in all societies affected by cultural press, exerted especially through adult urging, and cultural pull, made effective especially through rewards. Baby talk is neither a universal language, nor is it mainly invented by babies and young children. However, the baby-talk patterns of a particular culture may be highly persistent, as they have been shown to be in the Mediterranean area.

In large and complex societies there are linguistic subcultures varying with education, occupation, and socioeconomic status. It is reported that the working-class "restricted code" and the middle- and upper-class "elaborated code" usages are already apparent in the language culture of English children by age five. Studies in the United States confirm and support these findings. Though the relation between language and thought is not well understood, it is evident that value orientations and cognitive style are closely linked with language and that children in ethnic and in lower-class subsocieties may be linguistically ill-equipped for achievement in the nonethnic and middle-class schools. However, bilingualism as such is by no means a cognitive handicap, and it may indeed be an asset.

NOTES

[1] M. M. Lewis, *Language, Thought and Personality in Infancy and Childhood* (New York: Basic Books, 1963), p. 13.

[2] Lois N. Hoffman and Martin L. Hoffman, eds., *Review of Child Development Research* (New York: Russell Sage Foundation, 1966), II, 65.

[3] *Ibid.*, p. 67.

[4] William Stern, *Psychology of Early Childhood* (London: George Allen & Unwin Ltd., 1924), p. 164.

[5] Joseph Church, *Language and the Discovery of Reality* (New York: Random House, 1961) p. 62.

[6] *Ibid.*, p. 63.

[7] Hoffman and Hoffman, *op. cit.*, p. 72.

[8] Hildred Geertz, *The Javanese Family* (New York: The Free Press of Glencoe, 1961), p. 100.

[9] Sister M. Inez Hilger, *Arapaho Child Life and Its Cultural Background* (Washington, D.C.: Bureau of American Ethnology, Bulletin 148, 1952), pp. 41 f.

[10] Sister M. Inez Hilger, *Chippewa Child Life and Its Cultural Background* (Washington, D.C.: Bureau of American Ethnology, 1951), pp. 107 f.

[11] M. M. Lewis, *How Children Learn to Speak* (London: George G. Harrap, 1957), p. 80.

[12] Charles A. Ferguson, "Baby Talk in Six Languages," *American Anthropologist*, 66 (1964), 103-114.

[13] *Ibid.*, p. 104.

[14] Gibson A. Todd and Bruce Palmer, "Social Reinforcement of Infant Babbling," *Child Development*, 39 (1968), 595.

[15] Hoffman and Hoffman, *op. cit.*, p. 81.

[16] Roger Brown and Ursula Bellugi, "Three Processes in the Child's Acquisition of Syntax," *Harvard Educational Review*, 34 (1964), 144.

[17] Hoffman and Hoffman, *op. cit.*, p. 93.

[18] *Ibid.*, p. 93.

[19] *Ibid.*, p. 95.

[20] *Ibid.*, p. 91.

[21] Marion Blank and Frances Solomon, "A Tutorial Language Program to Develop Abstract Thinking in Socially Disadvantaged Preschool Children," *Child Development*, 39 (1968), 379 f. (italics original).

[22] *Ibid.*, p. 381.

[23] Joseph Church, *Three Babies—Biographies of Cognitive Development* (New York: Random House, 1966), p. 289.

[24] Church, *Language and the Discovery of Reality*, p. 209.

[25] Margaret E. Hertzig, Herbert G. Birch, Alexander Thomas, and Olga Aran Mendez, "Class and Ethic Differences in the Responsiveness of Preschool Children to Cognitive Demands," *Monographs of the Society for Research in Child Development*, 33 (1968), 46.

[26] *Ibid.*, p. 47.

[27] Hoffman and Hoffman, *op. cit.*, p. 90.

[28] A. Richard Diebold, Jr., "The Consequences of Early Bilingualism in Cognitive Development and Personality Formation," in Edward Norbeck, Douglass Price-Williams, and William M. McCord, eds., *The Study of Personality* (New York: Holt, Rinehart & Winston, 1968), p. 235.

[29] E. Peal and W. E. Lambert, "The Relation of Bilingualism to Intelligence," *Psychological Monographs*, No. 546 (1962), p. 20.

Self and Others: Identities, Differentiations, and Attitudes in Early Childhood

All life is an echo of our first sensations,
and we build up our consciousness, our
whole mental life, by variations and combinations of these elementary sensations,
. . . not only (of) colors and tones and
shapes, but also (of) patterns and atmospheres. . . .

Herbert Read

Nearly every adult can recall, from his very early childhood, some scene or moment. Autobiographies supply glimpses of the child's world of perceptions, though memory seldom preserves more than shadowy pictures, time-fogged mental snapshots.

An elderly Winnebago Indian woman recalls riding on her mother's back as mother and child and elder sister crossed a fast-flowing little creek. The details are vivid in her mind's eye: the swirling water, the older sister walking ahead, holding up her skirt. The baby, on whom all this made an indelible impression, was not yet two. Years later she asked her mother if the incident was real. It was; her mother thought she must have remembered because she had been frightened.[1]

In his autobiography author W. H. Hudson, who was born on the South American pampas, tells us:

All that I remember of my early life at this place comes between the ages of three or four or five; . . . to the eye of memory [it] appears like a wide

25

plain blurred over with a low-lying mist, with here and there a group of trees, a house, a hill, or other large object, standing out in the clear air with marvellous distinctness.[2]

Hudson remembered sunset, and great herds of cattle heading homeward through clouds of dust. And he remembered his mother watching her children at their before-bedtime play, a book in her lap and a smile on her face.

Norbert Wiener, late distinguished mathematician, recalled in his autobiography the scenes of his childhood at about the age of two. He and his parents lived then in a second-story apartment. The staircase leading to it "seemed to run from what was for me an interminable distance." Neighborhood scenes too remained in his mind's eye: "a confusion of streets" and "the acute angle at which these streets intersected before our particular grocery shop."[3]

A. L. Rowse, poet and historian, sketches a "picture in the mind" preserved, he thinks, from when he was three or younger. It is breakfast time, a winter morning in Cornwall. A lighted lamp stands on the kitchen table, and near it a "large enamel blue teapot." He remembers his vantage point, a "high-up baby's chair with the little tray attached in front. . . ."[4]

Self and Identity

Whether or not remembered, it is likely that early perceptions of one's physical and social surroundings were in their time vivid, and that many left their mark. Herbert Read's statement (quoted at the head of this chapter) is both profound and thoroughly in accord with what psychologists can tell us. Even consciousness of bodily self—that anchor point of becoming a sentient being—grows because "the infant receives a constant stream of organic sensations. . . ."[5] But "the sense of self depends on more than the bodily me," Gordon Allport adds.[6] It depends heavily on language—on labels for self and others, for own and other persons' possessions. In his second year of life the child speaks and thinks increasingly with the aid of linguistic tools.

The most important linguistic aid of all is the child's own name. He hears constantly "Where is Johnny's nose?" "Where are Johnny's eyes?" "Good Johnny," "John naughty." By hearing his name repeatedly the child gradually sees himself as a distinct and recurrent point of reference. The name acquires significance for him in the second year of life. With it comes awareness of independent status in the social group.[7]

However, such emphasis on the personal name is stronger in the United States than in some other societies. The emphasis may promote the development of a concept of self, but the concept is not dependent upon it. American children often reflect our personal name usage by referring to themselves by their own names: "this is Susie's doll"; "Johnny's tricycle." Young Japanese children, reflecting a very sparing use of personal names in their society, do nothing of the sort. They seldom refer to the self at all, either by name or by possessive pronoun ("my sister," "my book," etc.), yet the sense of self is probably on the average as clear and strong as it is among American children.

Along with self-awareness comes awareness of others, and assertion of self in opposition to others—the "no! no!" stage. At two years a child is likely to show his maximum of this "oppositional behavior," but its beginnings are apparent in many children by eighteen months. This is probably no news to parents of young children. Some of them know also that negativism may persist until the age of four, as psychiatrist D. M. Levy has reported.[8]

The general nature and meaning of major social categories—parents, siblings, other kin, non-kin—ordinarily are known to young children, who know also the linguistic labels for these categories. By age two a child of the Bantu-speaking Chaga (East Africa) knows such labels, accompanying personal names, and appropriate attitude and etiquette as well.

The first step in this direction was made when the parents reacted to the babbled syllables of *ta* and *ma*. Soon these words assume . . . a particular significance . . . a sense of obligation on the child's part, an admission of submissiveness toward parents . . . The first polite distinction is that between the personal names and the terms of address of his parents. . . . [Later] the more complicated kinship terminology is learned, . . . [and] a set of polite expressions useful in definite situations . . . [for example] the phrase *huu*, used when presenting a gift or handing over food. . . .[9]

In any society the three-year-old knows his own identity as a boy or a girl and he is rapidly learning what is considered appropriate behavior for boys and girls, for men and women. Even so, he may be quite willing, for another two years or so, to play games or perform chores that in his culture are generally the domain of the opposite sex. From age three or earlier he is likely to be curious about sex organs, and to learn very soon to sex-classify the people around him on the basis of body structures. But, according to psychologists Stone and Church, "at age four, even those children who know about

27

genital differences between boys and girls regard them as secondary to styles of coiffure or dress in determining sex and sex differences." They add this little story to make their point:

One four-year-old, visiting a family new to the neighborhood, observed their small baby creeping about the sunny lawn in the nude. Reporting on the new family to her mother, she was asked whether the baby was a boy or a girl, and replied, "I don't know. It's so hard to tell at that age, especially with their clothes off."[10]

A four-year-old is likely to have a strong sense of self. Now, "being firmly convinced that he is a person," he fumbles toward developing and refining his view of himself. Erik Erikson says that "he begins to make comparisons and is apt to develop untiring curiosity about differences."[11] He is likely to be sensitive to nuances of appearance and behavior. It is as though he had antennae constantly picking up, while his mind stores away, subtleties that the adults around him may believe him to have missed.

Having studied four- and five-year-olds in America and in Japan, I have seen for myself how keen are the perceptions and how sharp the logic they bring to bear on the social scene. They take note of people, things, and behavior, and they arrive at, or try out, classifications on the basis of these perceptions.

Others: Differentiations and Attitudes in the Japanese Culture of Early Childhood

My information about the Japanese culture of early childhood comes from an intensive study of 300 urban, middle-class five-year-olds (150 boys and 150 girls) made in the cities of Osaka and Kyoto under my direction.[12] Each of the children was interviewed at his or her kindergarten four times by a Japanese member of the research team. We used pretested interview schedules to ensure uniform coverage, and we adapted the interview method to young children by structuring it around pictures.

The pictures were not used as test devices, but rather to focus the child's attention on the social world, and to stimulate him to express to us his concepts and attitudes concerning it. In the first interview the subject was asked to draw pictures of a child, a woman, and a man. Then he was asked to tell us, about his own pictures, "what kind of person is this?" "what does this kind of person do?" "how do you feel about this kind of person—do you like or not like him (her)?" In the second interview we showed the child ten social-situation pictures. These we had selected from a Japanese edition of the *Thematic Apperception Test*—a picture series widely used as a diagnostic tool in personality studies, but used in our study only to stimulate the child to express his ideas about the social world. Our third and fourth interviews were built around twenty color-touched line drawings prepared for us by Japanese artists. These pictures represented a variety of social types: elderly and middle-aged Japanese, male and female, of lower-, middle-, and upper-class status (status suggested by the artist in the clothing, accessories, and grooming of the individual represented in each drawing); middle-aged, middle-class males and females of four other nationalities—American, Korean, Indian (of India), and Chinese (nationality suggested by the artist in the physiognomy and coloring, the clothing, accessories, and hair style of the individual represented in each drawing). These nationalities were represented, rather than others, because they are most likely to be a part of the social world in which the urban Japanese child lives.

In all interviews, as in the first, the child was asked to tell us about the "kind" of person in the picture, about what this kind of person does, and how he feels about this kind of person. What we learned from the children is a product of 1,200 interviews (four interviews with each of 300 subjects) and a total of almost 14,000 identifications made in response to the question "what kind of person is this (in the picture at hand)?"

In the social world around him, as an urban Japanese five-year-old sees it, there are people divided into several very general age/sex kinds; for example: old person, woman, man, grownup, young person, child, girl, boy, baby. But his world is dominated by immediate family members. "Mother" is front and center on his stage of life. Father is not far behind. Elder sister and grandmother are likely to figure importantly, followed by elder brother and grandfather. Aunt and uncle may be important. He is most attentive to the nurturing females of his family, and other females of the appropriate ages he inclines to see as motherlike, or as elder sisterlike, or as grandmotherlike.

This inclination to see non-kin as kinlike is characteristically Japanese. These children preserve a traditional culture's emphasis on kinship; they see their world of people as made up predominantly of kinfolk, real or pseudo. When a Japanese five-year-old points to the picture of an elderly woman and says "that's *obā-san*" (grandmother), the child is in all probability perfectly well aware that this is not the of-our-house/family (not the *uchi no*) grandmother. He is identifying the pictured woman in terms of age-sex

29

status and role. American children do this too—"that's a grandmother" (in the picture)—but the inclination is much less marked. Japanese children more frequently identify pictured persons in terms of kinship, real or pseudo, than in any other terms.

Little Japanese boys and girls see females in general as relatively mild, gentle, and kind. Males, particularly adult males of the father age and type, they see as rather formidable, even frightening (*kowai*). Mothers, or mother-type females, are not thought of as either well dressed or well groomed; it is the elder sister type they see as stylish, pretty, and "playing" or perhaps doing something nice for them. She may also work, at home or elsewhere. Mother types are expected to be busy mainly with domestic chores, especially with preparing food or doing the laundry, and so are elderly women— grandmothers and grandmother types.

The Japanese child thinks of mature men of the father type as people who work; perhaps they "go to the company." It is this work association that stands out above all others in children's concepts of the mature male and his activities. They think of elderly men as somewhat more likely to be "playing," but often the child thinks of them too as busy with some kind of work. Young men—elder-brother kind—are persons who go to school, study, do work (nondomestic), and who "play."

Language usage and other aspects of cultural tradition of course go far to shape the child's picture of his social world, as the extended use of kin terms has illustrated. In Japan there are other striking illustrations, the matter of relationships with siblings, for example.

Japanese neither conceive nor speak of "sister" or "brother" as such. In their language sibling terms always denote relative age, that is, elder or younger sister, elder or younger brother. Moreover, the kin terms referring to elder sister/brother are very commonly extended; the terms for younger sister/brother are not. In our many long talks with the children they made strikingly few references to younger siblings. For about half the 300 children we studied this would be due to the fact that they have no younger siblings, but the preoccupation with older siblings, and with older sibling types, undoubtedly reflects three cultural facts: the linguistic practice of extending the terms "elder sister" and "elder brother" (*onēsan* and *onīsan*) beyond their own big sisters and brothers and using them as labels for what American children might refer to as "big girls" and "big boys"; the Japanese practice of expecting big sisters and brothers (the sisters especially) often to look after the family's little children; finally, the traditional prestige of elder as compared with younger siblings in the Japanese family.

The five-year-old reflects another aspect of language and tradition when he specifies, as he quite often does, his view of some people as *yoso no*—"outside." He conceives also of a general category and of specific *uchi no* "inside" kin. Both *uchi no* and *yoso no* have social as well as spatial connotations. An *uchi no* person is thought of as inside and the *yoso no* person as outside both the family circle and the house. These linguistic devices make it easy to differentiate between, as it were, "inside" and "outside" people, and little children do so. *Yoso no ojisan*—an "uncle" not of our family or house—is frequently mentioned when the child looks at pictures of mature men. *Yoso no* grandmother, father, mother, grandfather, elder brother, and, rather rarely, elder sister identifications are made. In the child's-eye view of the world of people, the dichotomy between of-our-family/not-of-our family is sharp and important.

On the wider social stage the Japanese five-year-old is aware of a large number of occupational statuses. The doctor is especially important to him, but he shows interest too in a great many varieties of "shopkeeper." In a land where small and specialized shops are commonplace it is not surprising that the children we studied are aware, between them, of more than fifty different kinds of shopkeepers. Nor is it surprising (some aspects of childhood *are* world wide) that these children are interested especially in the sweet-shopkeeper and the toy-shopkeeper.

The urbanism of their world these children perceive in terms of a variety of roles. The American "organization man" has his Japanese parallel in the "company person," and to the Japanese five-year-old he is a familiar type. Some five-year olds are aware of men in related roles: "president of the company," "worker," and "laborer." Some know about "restaurant-keepers" and "innkeepers"; a good many are aware of entertainers (dancers, singers, etc.), of wrestlers and baseball players, of bus, train, and taxi drivers and conductors. Some of the children conceive of the "city person," and some know of another world—the world of farmers and of the "country person."

Many children perceive, on their social horizons, several kinds of people involved in what an adult would call "the educational system." They are of course particularly aware of kindergarten children *(yochien no)* and of themselves as a part of the kindergarten social world. They think of older children as "middle-school-going-persons," "university-going-persons," or just as students. In the "learned person" *(sensei)* category it is teachers who figure importantly for the child.

Two major spheres of human activity the Japanese child almost ignores are the military and the religious. Even passing mention of soldier or sailor is very rare, and of the priest, the "temple person," and the *Kami sama* (a term covering a variety of supernaturals in human form) as well. The reasons are apparent: Japan's postwar revulsion against militarism and all its works and workers, and the nation's strongly and primarily secular interests.

Certain unusual features of their social geography notwithstanding, the Japanese children talk and think largely in ways familiar to close observers of American children. Many of the Japanese are aware of rich and poor, of good and bad persons, of policemen, burglars, and beggars, of housemaids, friends, and guests. The "great person," the "sick" or "hurt person," the "neighborhood person," "the person of Japan," even the generic "human being" figure in the thinking of some of the Japanese children.

So do characters from folk tales, legends, and children's stories. Snow White is known and loved, along with *Momotaro* (Little Peach Boy) whose story nearly every little Japanese has heard from infancy. The princess *(ohimesama)* is a great favorite with little girls. The prince, the feudal lord or his retainer, even the generalized "person of antiquity" *(mukashi no hito)* play significant parts in the child world as it is peopled out of stories and out of the past. Real and living royalty seems to figure not at all in the thinking of these little children.

Japanese children are very much interested in Americans *(Americajin; Amerika no hito)*, whom they know by that name or as *Shinchugun*—occupational force personnel—or *Haro* (Hello). Americans were in fact very few in Osaka and Kyoto at the time of the study (1955), and Koreans were overwhelmingly numerous (95 percent) among foreigners in those cities, yet it was mainly about the Americans that the children talked. A large majority (almost three-fourths) of the 300 youngsters we studied used the label "American" at least once, and a third of them spoke of no foreign type except the American. Only five children know of British, English, or French people. Indians (of India) and Koreans were known to many more, but still to relatively few as compared with those aware of Americans.

Genus Americanus is to be recognized, so the children tell us, primarily by the hair and the eyes and the face, and secondarily by his clothing. Somewhat surprisingly, the size of the creature, which might be expected to impress the children in a nation of relatively small people, seldom comes in for comment. But the "yellow" or "brown" hair, the "blue" or "water-color" (literal translation) or "different" eyes, and the "American" or "not-like-Japanese" face are much commented upon. So are the "American" or "beautiful" or "nice" clothes of this remarkable creature.

What the American does with his (or her) time, and where he does it, appears to be for the children a rather perplexing matter. They know very well what Japanese of many social categories do, and where, and that the number-one activity for Japanese is work and more work, of many varieties. Japanese boys, girls, and young women of the elder sister category are seen as exceptions to this rule, it is true, but with these exceptions the social world populated by Japanese is seen as primarily industrious. But Americans seem to be primarily engaged in "play" activities of one sort or another. Such work as is occasionally associated with them is of a vague and unspecified order except for the household chores, which the children assume that even American women must sometimes do. However, it is only the American, among mature females foreign or otherwise, who is thought of as primarily occupied with recreation; all other adult women are seen as first and foremost occupied with work, and especially with domestic tasks.

What the children often call the "play" activities of Americans include a variety of doings connoting leisure and recreation. Among these doings nothing looms so prominently to the Japanese children as this foreigner's "going"; he is seen as forever "going out" or "going somewhere." More explicitly, he is thought of as "going to some nice place," "going to Osaka Castle" (that is, sightseeing), "going to Daimaru" (or another department store), "going everywhere." With respect to American women there is much talk of "going shopping," for example: "she is always shopping—" "she goes to look at gloves and shoes—" And there seems to be a widespread notion that, in addition to shopping, American women spend much of their time in dancing and in such other colorful activities as these:

"She always borrows the house of 'Haro' (that is, Mr. Hello), and sleeps there."

"She drinks sake—"

"She walks into a bar, and speaks to men."

Through the eyes of the children we see the Americans strolling about in leisurely fashion bent on sightseeing or shopping or a quest for entertainment, or alternately we see them whizzing about in cars or *jipu* (jeeps), or on planes. Whatever the rate or the mode, the American is seen as perpetually in motion.

In addition to his "play" and his vaguely conceived "work," the

33

children are of the opinion that the American may occupy himself with activities of a hostile-aggressive-warlike nature. Comments to this effect are fewer than those dealing with the American's play and work, but frequent enough to show us that the Japanese child does not always see the American as either benign or harmless. The American "makes war," "shoots the gun," "saves money and will buy a gun when the next war breaks out," and the female of the species "grows her fingernails long and scratches others!" One little Japanese boy declares: "I don't want to go to America, because those people have guns."

Among the modalities of expressions with respect to the activities of Americans the fourth most frequent has to do with communication. The American talks and sings and writes "in English, and *not* in Japanese." In connection with other kinds of foreigners language is almost never mentioned; in the minds of the children Americans alone are associated with a babble "which I don't understand."

Among the children there are two clear-cut schools of thought with respect to Americans, a positive and a negative. These two have about equal numbers of adherents so far as the American male is concerned, but the female wins twice as many positive as negative votes, and is indeed far and away the most popular of foreign types. (Apparently the children's concept of her rather frivolous and garish life by no means offends them.) The American male, though liked by no more than half the children, still comes out second best in the popularity poll when other foreigners, male and female, are included.

The children showed themselves entirely ready, willing, and able to provide us with reasons for their likes and dislikes. Among their reasons for liking American men two major modes appear: (1) they like them because of the things these men do, especially the "buys me—gives me—" kinds of doings; (2) they like them because of the "nice" or "good" clothing they wear. American women are liked especially because of their "pretty" "beautiful" clothes or jewelry, and secondarily because they themselves are regarded as "pretty" and generally attractive.

For not liking Americans, male and female, two kinds of reasons are most frequently given: (1) the sheer fact that the individual *is* American, that is, dislike for Americans as such, usually without further explanation; (2) the fact that the American speaks English, a matter which is found objectionable of itself, or because "I don't understand." Features of personal appearance, clothing, and behavior are "not like" reasons less frequently advanced but by no means negligible.

34

Besides expressing his like/not like feelings with respect to Americans, each child also told us what he thought he might do if he were to meet one of these creatures face to face. The comments fell into two major categories, which we label, respectively, "acceptance" and "avoidance/rejection," in reference to the attitudes implied by the comments.

Apparently, it may be one thing to feel favorably disposed toward Americans and ready to declare a liking for them, but something else again to imagine yourself actually having anything to do with them. So, we conclude from the lesser frequency of acceptance responses than of "I like" declarations that fewer than half the children indicate acceptance attitudes, and in about half the cases, the statements suggest nothing more than that minimal acceptance implied by observing the amenities. Avoidance/rejection responses are a little more frequent than those of the acceptance type, but these are more often of the avoidance sort, suggesting minimal negativism, than of the rejection sort.

But if the children are given to reservations about contacts with Americans, they are very much more so inclined where other foreigners are concerned. Again we find the children implying that Americans stand in a relatively, if not absolutely, high place on their scale of esteem.

Often the responses which we have called accepting are merely polite greetings. For example, the child tells us: "I would say 'good morning'/'good day' to the American, or "I would make a bow," or "I would say 'Amerika San' (literally, 'Mr. America'), "or perhaps I would say 'Haro!' " Minimal as this kind of acceptance is, it suggests a social stance at once polite and by no means unfriendly.

Verbal gestures suggesting a considerably more committal stance come from fewer (about one-fifth) of the children. However, such statements often demonstrate an eager readiness to accept the American, his company, and his favors. For example:

"(I would like to) go somewhere together (with the American)."

"—Go with him to his house."

"—Ride on an airplane with him."

"—Have him take me to the park."

"(I would) be glad to meet him; would have him take me to America."

"Would have a talk/have him teach me English."

"Would ask him to give gum/to take my picture."

"Would get *okashi* (sweets)/get ten *yen*."

As we have noted above, the more or less friendly stances suggested by the children's comments are somewhat less frequent than those of a more or less negativistic sort. What we have called avoidance responses are very common even among children who declare that they like Americans. Avoidance is often a matter simply of inaction on the child's part (as he anticipates his behavior in meeting an American); he would "keep silent" or "do nothing." It may also be a matter of making a show of indifference; the child would "make a don't-know face," thereby utilizing in this situation an idiom of culturally patterned expression appropriate to situations seen as ill-defined, as unattractive, or both.

Rejection responses are largely statements that suggest that the child finds the American so unattractive or so fearsome that his one thought would be to beat a hasty retreat; the child would "go away," "run home," or "hide." An occasional child, perhaps more bold or hostile, would stand his ground and speak his mind in no uncertain terms, or perhaps "beat her" or "fight him." The most audacious would say "fool of an American," or express the sentiment not uncommon among peoples who have served as reluctant hosts to visitors from the United States; he would say, "Go back to America!"

For some children the echoes of war are still reverberating, and the American is the man with the gun; he is the fighter, or he is the fighter who became "occupation force personnel."

Our study of social differentiations and attitudes in the urban Japanese culture of early childhood supports these conclusions:

1. The child sees a wide social world around him, a world divided into age/sex, occupational, foreign/nonforeign, and other kinds of people; however, it is the members of his family who hold the front and center places on his stage of life.

2. With each of the many social kinds he recognizes, the child associates particular types of activities and personality characteristics.

3. The child's social categorizations and attitudes are linked with and affected by his language and the differentiations it allows or prescribes.

4. Certain social types—Americans, for example—occupy the attention and interest of children to an extent quite out of proportion to their numbers in the social world around him; this finding suggests that events of overriding importance to adults—the war and the American occupation, for example—inevitably will be reflected in the culture of childhood.

It is reasonable to suppose that similar studies in other societies would lead to similar conclusions, though cultural differences would be apparent. The Japanese five-year-old's special interest in and awareness of the members of his own household would no doubt be paralleled in most urban settings. However, the facility with which he differentiates between kin, kinlike, and non-kin persons would not be paralleled in societies whose languages do not invite these or other language-based differentiations. The breadth of the Japanese child's social perceptions, the multiplicity of social types of which he is aware, and about which he holds concepts and attitudes, we would expect to find paralleled in urban middle-class children of all contemporary societies. We would expect also that, as in Japan, recent and current events that occupy the adults of a society would be reflected in that society's culture of early childhood.

Others: Race Differentiation and Attitudes in the U.S. Culture of Early Childhood

Young children quite naturally are struck first by the more conspicuous features of people, and the more conspicuous differences between them. Size differences, sex differences, and what the adult world calls "race" differences are apparent to them, and intriguing.

By the third year of his life the [Negro] child is asking the kinds of questions that ultimately will include one about his skin color. A mother of five children in Jackson, Mississippi, . . . [said]: "When they asks all the questions, they ask about their color too. They more than not will see [they are likely to see] a white boy or girl, and it makes them stop and think."[13]

In racially integrated American nursery schools in New England, I recorded spontaneous comments that illustrate awareness of racial attributes in the self and in others. Carol observed thoughtfully: "See how colored my hands are." Herman commented, and quite correctly: "My mother's brown-skinned." Stefan said: "My mother's *that* white."

The children made racial classifications too. Thomas studied the children around him and said: "There are two white children here and all the rest are colored." It was a sophisticated comment; the "colored" included children who were very light. Norman one day asked his teacher, teasingly, she thought, "What color are you?" Sam answered for her: "She's brown." Norman agreed: "She's brown and I'm brown." This was more than simple description, because Mrs. D. is notably browner than Norman. Sam added: "Yes, and I'm brown too." He then named a number of children and teachers, not all of whom were present, correctly labeling each of them "white" or "brown" or "colored."

Hair form as well as skin color is a feature of interest, but it is a secondary basis for classification. In the nursery school Donald, Sam, and Norman discussed the hair of the children around them.

37

They said some (the Negro children) had "curly" hair and some (the white children) had "straight" or "curly-at-the-bottom" hair. Comments about hair—its form, color, length, and the style in which it is worn—are very common. The children stroke or finger one another's hair occasionally, when hands and heads happen to be in proximity. Deep interest is sometimes expressed by the way they do it. When they say that so-and-so is "white" and go on to explain "why," they rarely mention hair. The usual explanation is: "Because he has that kind of face (or hands, legs, eyes)." It is the unusual child who adds: "and he has white hair" (that is, the kind whites have).

Awareness of physical differences and identities is not always so objective or so neutral. The young child is likely to perceive not only that there are physical attributes in terms of which the self and others can be classified by age or sex or race. He is likely to perceive too that these physical attributes are unequally valued in his world of people. And "doing what comes naturally"—and almost inevitably—he picks up those prevalent patterns of differential valuing which he has observed. He does not need to be taught. He absorbs, by experiencing sensations of "patterns and atmospheres," just as Herbert Read said.

Given the long-standing American patterns of preference for racial whiteness over all other racial attributes, it is inevitable that many children will absorb these patterns. But there are two aspects of this situation which, though long and conclusively documented by numbers of independent studies, are still unknown to many parents and teachers, and surprising to them. One is that many white children not older than five are already quite racially "prejudiced." The other is that many Negro children of this age are already aware of the prejudices of whites, and that they share these feelings to such an extent that they are at best highly ambivalent about the racial attributes of the self. At worst they reject the racial self, with heat, as did the little Negro girl in my study who exclaimed: "Black people —I hate 'em!" And on another occasion, as she picked up a brown doll: "This one, this one I'm holding, it just gets on my nerves."[14]

Researchers report again and again that young Negro children will identify themselves quite correctly as "colored," or "brown," or "black," but they do so reluctantly and with evident discomfort and emotional strain. "Many Negro citizens apparently learn by three years of age that skin color is important, that white is to be desired, dark to be regretted." So C. Landreth and B. C. Johnson conclude on a basis of their study in California.[15] Kenneth Clark, pioneer in research of this kind, writes:

Among three-year-old Negro children in both northern and southern communities, more than 75% showed that they were conscious of the difference between "white" and "colored" . . . This knowledge develops in stability and clarity from year to year, and by the age of seven it is a part of the knowledge of all Negro children. Other investigators . . . have shown that the same is true of white children.[16]

The child's first awareness of racial differences is . . . associated with some rudimentary evaluation of these differences. . . . [Moreover], the child . . . cannot learn what racial group he belongs to without being involved in a larger pattern of emotions, conflicts, and desires which are part of his growing knowledge of what society thinks about his race.[17]

Children who are racially Mongoloid are affected by such knowledge too. This fact has been reported from Hawaii, where whites are less generally superordinate than they are on the mainland, and nonwhite children might therefore be freer of tendencies to disvalue their own physical attributes. But three- to six-year-old "Oriental" children who experience close association with whites in biracial schools show significantly more "white preference" than do Oriental youngsters who attend school with other Orientals only.[18]

To see race differences through the eyes of a young child, and to know something of the feelings that accompany his perceptions, requires close observation, thorough acquaintance, and opportunities for leisurely private talks with the child. Busy with other concerns, even parents and nursery school teachers may miss many of the hints the child throws out, or would throw out, if given encouragement to do so in a private setting. The researcher meets the necessary conditions and often discovers what parents and teachers did not guess—that the child is highly aware of and sensitive to matters involving race.

Sarah, who is white, is an excellent example. At her nursery school there were a few Negro children, and one Negro teacher. But week after week Sarah's behavior at school gave no indication that she either noticed or cared about color. Yet the researcher's report on her behavior during the play interviews (the four private sessions we held with each child) reads as follows: Awareness of race differences is accurate and verbalized. She is clearly aware of what she calls 'black people' and has rather strong feelings about them. She shows a rather consistent rejection of Negroes."

The case of Joan, who is not white, points up the discrepancy between what her mother knew of her awareness and what we came to know. At home Joan had once referred to a nursery school child as "white," and she had once asked whether a certain other friend was "white." That was all, so far as her mother's observations went. But alone with the researcher Joan repeatedly described and labeled dolls or pictured people as "white" or "brown" or "colored." She volunteered comments about real people too: "My Daddy's colored." "My Mommy's colored." Most notable of all was her thoughtful comment as she carefully arranged the brown and the white figures in a puzzle board. "The people that are white, they can go up. The people that are brown, they have to go down." Joan was not yet four and a half, but her comment strikes the adult ear as a capsule statement of historic race relations in American society.[19]

The American situation has a remarkably close parallel in the Republic of South Africa. A recent study of white and Bantu children in that country was conducted to test four hypotheses derived from U.S. studies. The white children (30 of them) are between five and seven years old. The Bantu children (139) are between three and seven. Seventy-four of the Bantu children live in a city; the rest are rural dwellers. The researchers conclude:

The results support the four hypotheses: (a) South African white children should, by the age of 5, manifest racial preferences which are consistently white orientated; (b) white South African children, identifying with the white ego-ideal characterized by physical traits of high visibility, should evidence an incipient rejection of outgroup members; (c) Bantu children in South Africa, as members of a prestige-deprived minority (the term "minority" is used to denote a qualitative and not a quantitative concept), should be outgroup orientated, evincing preference for, and attempting an indentification with, the valued white ideal; (d) because protracted interracial contact during early stages in ego development involves the child in a more emphatic conflict of identities than in a noninterracial-contact situation, it was expected that rural Bantu children, insulated from white contact, would give less evidence of identity confusion than would Bantu children.[20]

Invidious social distinctions are not limited to American society, nor to American child culture. There is a "widely held belief that ethnic relations (that is, relations between the indigenous Maori and the *pakeha* or whites) in New Zealand are more harmonious than are Negro-white relations in the United States."[21] However, numerous studies of Maori and *pakeha* children show that cross-ethnic awareness and attitudes are much like the cross-racial perceptions that have been observed in the United States. A majority of *pakeha* four-year-olds show unmistakable own-race preferences. Maori four-year-olds, like young Negro children, show a strong tendency toward other-race—toward whiteness—preferences.[22]

Child's-eye views of their own and others' religious and national identities have been studied only scantily in children younger than five. Distinctions of these sorts are neither as strongly marked in American society nor as self-evident as race differences. Probably children do not perceive religious or nationality differences either so early or so clearly. There is some evidence that those whose own identity is with a minority are inclined toward earlier awareness than are majority group children.[23] Jewish youngsters aged five to nine are reported to be more aware of this identity and to feel their ties with the group more strongly than either Protestant or Catholic children.[24]

In India, caste identities and rules are heavily emphasized parts of the culture of early childhood. It has been reported that "Every child imbibes caste prejudice before he takes his first steps. Never does he permit himself to be touched by one of the sweeper children. If in an unguarded moment he runs the risk of pollution, he is snatched to a zone of safety by a big sister or brother."[25]

In sum, the findings permit a number of generalizations. Out of the kaleidoscopic richness of his early sensations and sociocultural experiences, the little child acquires a concept and an image of self, and at the same time he is identifying the others around him. The culture of early childhood incorporates a system of social categories into which the little child places the others he knows or hears about. It also provides ready-made concepts and attitudes concerning persons who fall in categories such as class, race, sex, kin and non-kin, occupation, even individual qualities.

NOTES

[1] Nancy O. Lurie, *Mountain Wolf Woman* (Ann Arbor: University of Michigan Press paperback, 1966), pp. 1 f.

[2] W. H. Hudson, *Far Away and Long Ago* (New York: E. P. Dutton & Co.; London and Toronto: J. M. Dent & Sons, 1923), pp. 10 f.

[3] Norbert Wiener, *Ex-Prodigy* (Cambridge, Mass.: The Massachusetts Institute of Technology Press, 1964), pp. 31 f.

[4] A. L. Rowse, *A Cornish Childhood* (London: Jonathan Cape, 1942), p. 82.

[5] Gordon W. Allport, *Pattern and Growth in Personality* (New York: Holt, Rinehart & Winston, 1961), p. 113.

[6] *Ibid.*, p. 114.

[7] *Ibid.*, p. 115.

[8] D. M. Levy, "The Early Development of Independent and Oppositional Behavior," Chapter 5 in *Midcentury Psychiatry* (Springfield, Ill.: Charles C. Thomas, 1953).

[9] Otto Raum, *Chaga Childhood* (New York: Oxford University Press, 1940), pp. 169 f.

[10] L. Joseph Stone and Joseph Church, *Childhood and Adolescence* (New York: Random House, 1957), p. 165.

[11] Erik H. Erikson, "Growth and Crises of the 'Healthy Personality,' " in M. J. E. Senn, ed., *Problems of Infancy and Childhood* (New York: Josiah Macy Jr. Foundation, 1950), pp. 32 f.

[12] Mary Ellen Goodman, Y. Huzioka, and H. Matsuura, "Social Awareness in Young Children: A Study of Japanese Five-Year-Olds" (mimeographed, 1958).

[13] Robert Coles, *Children of Crisis* (Boston: Little, Brown and Co., 1967), p. 63.

[14] Mary Ellen Goodman, *Race Awareness in Young Children*, rev. ed. (New York: Collier Books, 1964).

[15] C. Landreth and B. C. Johnson, "Young Children's Responses to a Picture and Inset Test, . . ." *Child Development*, 24 (1953), p. 78.

[16] Kenneth B. Clark, *Prejudice and Your Child* (Boston: Beacon Press, 1955), p. 19.

[17] *Ibid.*, p. 23.

[18] Doris V. Springer, "Awareness of Racial Differences by Preschool Children in Hawaii," *Genetic Psychology Monographs*, 41 (1950), 215-270.

[19] Goodman, *Race Awareness in Young Children, passim.*

[20] A. J. Gregor and D. A. McPherson, "Racial Preference and Ego Identity Among White and Bantu Children in the Republic of South Africa," *Genetic Psychology Monographs*, 73 (1966), p. 247.

[21]Graham M. Vaughan, "The Development of Ethnic Attitudes in New Zealand School Children," *Genetic Psychology Monographs*, 70 (1964), p. 171.

[22]*Ibid., passim;* also Graham M. Vaughan, "Ethnic Awareness in Relation to Minority Group Membership," *The Journal of Genetic Psychology*, 105 (1964), pp. 119-130; Graham M. Vaughan and R.H.T. Thompson, "New Zealand Children's Attitudes Toward Maoris," *Journal of Abnormal and Social Psychology*, 62 (1961), pp. 701-704.

[23]E. L. Hartley, M. Rosenbaum, and S. Schwartz, "Children's Use of Ethnic Frames of Reference," *Journal of Psychology*, 26 (1948), pp. 367-368.

[24]Marlon Radke and J. Sutherland, "Children's Concepts and Attitudes About Minority and Majority American Groups," *Journal of Educational Psychology*, 40 (1949), pp. 449-468.

[25]William Wiser and Charlotte Wiser, *Behind Mud Walls* (Berkeley: University of California Press, 1963), p. 89.

4

Self and Others: Identities,
Differentiations, and Attitudes
in the Middle Years

The "middle years" are, for this discussion, roughly the years between age six and age thirteen. From age six or thereabout the child continues to expand and refine his concept of self, and of the relations between self and others. This requires also expansion and refinement of his concepts of others—their similiarities and differences. He becomes increasingly interested in others and their attributes from a fairly objective point of view. But the subjective view —the view of others as they affect and relate to the self—is probably never wholly outgrown in a long lifetime, much less in the middle years of childhood.

The growing interest in others, and a widening involvement with them, provides a basis for expanded horizons of perception and knowledge. Sex, age, occupational roles, morals, and values, all are patterned in his culture, and all are matters about which the child is likely to become well informed by the onset of puberty.

"Well informed" is, of course, a relative term. It is relative to culturally patterned expectations. It is relative to the sheer bulk of a culture's content—to how much there is to be learned, to be known. A child at the onset of puberty may be expected to know enough of his society's subsistence technology, and to have sufficiently practiced many of its techniques, to be nearly ready to assume full adult status with all its responsibilities. Such an expectation is entirely reasonable and even necessary when the total cultural content is small and the life expectancy short, as is the case among peoples dependent for subsistence on hunting and gathering (the contemporary South African Bushmen, for example) or on simple horticulture (for example, the contemporary tribes of interior highland New Guinea).

The Self

The people around a child, as they react to him, in effect hold up before him a mirror in which he sees himself. Moreover they constitute a social network in which he locates himself and establishes an identity. An Egyptian village child says: "I am the son of _____." The child's sense of personal worth is a facet of this identity. This Egyptian child, facing another boy, adds: "My father is better than yours; he never worked for someone else, and his turban has always been white."[1] A Puerto Rican child, living in a New York slum, can say: "I am just a little girl, nine years old, and don't know much, but I do know that I love Arturo, Grandma, Crucita and *mami* very much. *Mami* is good and gives me love." These affectional ties are the little girl's anchor points in an otherwise chaotic jumble of people: "I love my *mama* and will never leave her alone. And neither will she leave me."[2]

Against the yardsticks—the standards—provided by others the child learns to measure himself. Most children, upon perceiving the self as failing to measure up, will take steps, however reluctantly, toward making adjustments in the self. With rare exceptions (psychopaths, sociopaths, psychotics, neurotics, or the grossly educationally-deprived) children perceive significant discrepancies between the actual self and the dimensions of the self as it should be, if it were in accord with their culture's standards and expectations. They not only perceive discrepancies; they are made sufficiently anxious and uncomfortable to exert effort toward reshaping the self. "Every child . . . believes in the values of the world around him and thus starts by being, not a revolutionary, but an utter conservative."[3] Children want to be approved and rewarded for meeting expectations. They are likely to want approval and reward enough to overcome that universal human inertia that acts as a stabilizer. It serves to hold us on course, persisting in established patterns, barring strong deflecting pressures or competing inclinations.

Aspirations for the self, short range and long range, are likely to develop in the middle years along with self-image. There are likely to be several kinds of aspirations, differently weighted by the child in accord with his sex, age, and circumstances. In American society girls, much more than boys, are likely to aspire primarily to be desired and pursued by especially desirable members of the opposite sex. Boys, if exposed to the prevailing "achievement orientation"

46

of our culture, are likely to aspire primarily to economic success and to occupational roles of a prestigious sort. Children ordinarily perceive and reflect the aspirations prevalent among the adults around them and among their peers, especially those a little older than themselves. An American boy is unlikely to aspire, like boys among the New Guinea Gururumba, to be a "hot" man—a trigger-tempered aggressor only a little less violent among his tribal fellows than with outsiders. That aspiration reflects a rather unusual cultural view. But his personality goals, like his occupational aspirations, will almost surely reflect the ethics and values that the child perceives as prevalent in his world.

Self-Descriptions

"Imagine asking large numbers of children of different ages from a variety of different nations to answer the question, 'What are you?' "[4] What sort of answers might you get, and what national differences might appear? It would be difficult to guess what the responses might be. A remarkable recent study conducted by Wallace E. Lambert and Otto Klineberg has provided responses from urban six-, ten-, and fourteen-year-olds (100 of each age, 50 working- or lower-class, 50 middle-class) in eleven nations. The children were asked questions designed to elicit their views of foreign peoples as well as their views of themselves and people of their own nation.

Lambert and Klineberg found that self-descriptions were given predominantly in terms of sex, person (or human being), student, child, nation or region, religion, and race (see Table 1).[5] Emphasis on sex identity was quite variable among national and age groups. Americans and English-Canadians especially were apt to describe themselves first as "boy" or "girl," even at age fourteen. French-Canadians, French, Germans, and Brazilians shared this American-English inclination at the ages of six or ten, but at fourteen they tended to think of themselves as students. Turkish children, more than others, thought of themselves first as persons, and a little less frequently as students, children, boys or girls. The Japanese emphasized nation or region, and the Bantu—at age ten especially—emphasized race.

These findings contrast sharply the extent to which a child's-eye view, even the child's view of himself, is a matter of culture. It is of course also a matter of intellectual maturity (which is itself a matter of more than age, and of sophistication—of acquired knowledge and perspective). Maturation rates and degrees of sophistication are not unaffected by culture, to be sure. But the impact of

Table 1. Popular Categories of Response to the Four Questions Asking "What are you?"

(Table entries are percentages)

	Sex				Person				Student				Child				National or Regional				Religion				Race			
	Over-all	Age 6	10	14	Over-all	Age 6	10	14	Over-all	Age 6	10	14	Over-all	Age 6	10	14	Over-all	Age 6	10	14	Over-all	Age 6	10	14	Over-all	Age 6	10	14
American	21	21	22	20	11	9	11	13	2	3	2	3	3	2	1	4	5	2	4	8	2	1	2	3	0	0	0	0
Bantu	12	7	12	17	11	4	13	14	5	2	0	5	10	8	10	10	0	0	1	0	0	0	0	0	14	9	22	13
Brazilian	17	16	20	14	6	8	6	5	4	1	4	12	1	1	3	3	2	2	2	3	4	2	4	5	0	0	0	0
English-Canadian	20	16	21	24	11	8	14	10	6	1	3	12	4	5	4	4	5	2	5	7	3	2	4	4	0	0	0	0
French	12	14	15	8	5	1	7	7	4	4	13	14	6	5	9	4	6	2	6	10	1	0	1	0	0	0	0	0
French-Canadian	19	23	17	17	4	3	6	4	12	2	14	18	5	6	7	2	4	2	6	4	2	0	3	2	0	0	0	0
German	18	21	21	13	9	9	13	10	7	7	15	16	8	13	9	4	8	4	8	11	2	2	3	3	0	0	0	0
Israeli*	0	0	0	0	11	8	12	11	8	7	8	10	23	21	22	26	20	1	29	30	4	3	2	6	0	0	0	0
Japanese	10	2	13	14	4	9	1	1	0	0	0	0	1	2	3	1	1	0	1	0	1	0	2	1	0	0	0	0
Lebanese	11	9	12	12	5	2	7	7	2	2	12	15	2	2	3	2	10	1	6	10	9	9	13	6	0	0	0	0
Turkish	11	9	8	15	16	12	15	22	15	10	15	19	12	17	13	7	9	6	9	12	6	2	8	7	0	0	0	0

*In Hebrew there is no way to separate references made to sex and child. That is, if an Israeli boy says he's a "child," he also indicates that he's a male child. Because of this inevitable linkage, all such responses have been arbitrarily placed in the child category but are not interpreted as such.

cultures is most evident when children's self-descriptions reflect what we know to be national preoccupations—that is, sex in America, national unity in Japan, race in South Africa. Moreover, these emphases are likely to be persistent; " . . . self-references reflect cultural values that in turn influence behavior,"[6] thereby perpetuating the emphases.

Self and Others

By age six a child will be quite sophisticated about who's who in his immediate social proximity, and his awareness may extend well beyond that world.

Kin vs. non-kin, male vs. female, old (parents' or grandparents') vs. young (own and siblings' generation), important vs. unimportant —these social categories at least will be understood. The understanding will be accompanied by well-learned patterns of interpersonal behavior. The child knows how he should or may behave toward, or in the presence of, these various categories of people.

Until quite recently, as mankind's history goes, it would have been difficult to find a society lacking clear definition of intergenerational relations. It would have been almost as difficult to find one in which elders were not quite generally superordinate, a situation entirely in accord with culturally patterned expectations. Contemporary urban industrial societies—notably the United States, Sweden, and England—are in these respects cultural anomalies (as measured against the cultures of man's long past). In these three societies, and other modern societies that are heirs to the Western European cultural tradition or influenced by that tradition (contemporary urban Japan), adult-child relations are on the whole shifting, and poorly defined. The Western cultures are unusual too in another way, as adults' and children's rights and prerogatives tend toward equalization, if not toward partial dominance of the young over their elders. A serious book entitled *Teen-Age Tyranny* would have been most unlikely anywhere in the world before the post-World War II years. Its appearance in the United States in 1963 caused no great stir.[7] It is only one of a flood of books and lesser publications devoted to analysis and comment on the roles—actual and desirable—of the young versus their elders. The significant point is that the matter is debatable, and that it is indeed endlessly debated. In traditional cultures such ambiguities were unthinkable.

The mode of relationship prevalent for centuries in most human cultures is still dominant in what the modern world regards as "primitive" or "underdeveloped" societies. In his report on growing up in Silwa, an Egyptian village in the province of Aswan, Hamed Ammar provides an illustration.

... one of the cardinal virtues of a disciplined child is his respect for his elders. Till the age of four or five, this respect expresses itself in the young boy, on being introduced to a gathering in the house, touching the older person's hands with his lips and forehead. When the child grows older, this is replaced by a handshake followed immediately by his withdrawal from the adult gathering.[8]

Verbal intimacy and physical proximity between children and their parents or other elders decrease during the middle years, and an etiquette of deference prevails. The child never walks or rides in front or even abreast of his elders, he stands or at least assumes a "proper" sitting position when an elder approaches, he dismounts from his donkey when he comes in sight of his father in a formal gathering, and he observes many more rules of etiquette in attending to and serving guests.

Children know, however, that strict etiquette need not be observed when family members are alone and the occasion is neither public nor ceremonial. Informal situations permit "a certain amount of latitude," but none at all is allowed on formal occasions. Moreover, the child expects fewer opportunities for informality as he grows older. Through his behavior the child expresses, ideally at any rate, filial piety and submission. "Children's respect for and devotion to parents must be absolute and unconditional and do not have to be verbalized."[9]

Egyptian village children, like the urban Japanese five-year-olds my colleagues and I studied, learn kinship terms and identities during early childhood. Ammar reports:

... by the age of five, the children I spoke to were quite capable of telling the categories of paternal uncle and aunt, maternal uncle and aunt, cousins and nephews and nieces [and] ... what type of behaviour and sentiment is expected from him toward different relatives ... They also knew that their close relatives are those by whom they can be protected or punished, and whom they fear and love, and to whose houses they can stray, accepting food without fear of being punished by the parents ... Children use only eight terms of address: father, mother, grandfather, grandmother, paternal and maternal uncle and aunt.[10]

Whatever the prescribed patterns of behavior toward elders, and however faithfully the child may adhere to these prescriptions, his private sentiments do not necessarily match his overt behavior.

50

Individuality has its effects in all relationships in every society; children of the same parents very often have very different feelings toward those parents, even though they have been equally cared for and cherished.

Relationships are affected on the covert level also by a certain ambivalence that is probably an inevitable component of close human bonds. It has been said that ". . . in primitive society . . . there was commonly a feeling of hostility underlying the affection and gratitude children felt toward their parents."[11] This may be true, but it is probably no truer of "primitive" than of modern societies. Quite possibly the "hostility" component is on average greater and the "affection/gratitude" component lesser in our own and similar modern societies than among the "primitives." Certainly overt rebellion, hostility, and even physical assault directed by children toward parents and other elders are enormously more frequent in modern societies.

The sex of parent and of child will of course affect to some degree the child's sentiments. This is not to say that the supposed "Oedipal problem," or the parallel "Electra problem," need be involved. An anthropologist cannot accept as "universal" an aspect of behavior he knows to be lacking in even one society, and the famous "complex" seems to be quite absent from more than one. The Oedipus complex must remain in the category of nonuniversals.[12] Quite possibly it should be regarded as an aspect of abnormal rather than of normal relationships even in those societies in which something of the sort does occasionally appear. In light of anthropological data one must conclude that the whole "problem" has been grossly overemphasized by psychoanalytically-oriented scholars, some anthropologists included among them.[13]

The Oedipus argument has served to obscure what would seem an obvious and elemental fact of experience, a fact to which almost everyone can attest: one's sentiments toward both one's parents may be warm and deeply affectionate, but there will be a subtle qualitative difference in one's feelings toward same sex and opposite sex parent. This difference may of course assume decisive proportions, but ordinarily this is not the case. Anthropologists' reports show rather that the child's feelings usually assume essentially the culturally approved forms, and incestuous urges are almost never approved.

What is approved, and universally, is a role for mother and a different role for father. The associated role personalities inevitably differ, more or less in accord with role prescriptions. As a result, mothers ordinarily are unlike fathers vis-à-vis their children, by whom they are quite naturally perceived differently. Studies of children in the United States have shown that they think father's primary role to be "earning a living," mother's "homemaking." Mothers are generally perceived as "more 'nurturant,' 'nicer,' and more inclined to give presents than father." In these same studies father is perceived "as being more competent and punitive than mother and as being the more salient of the two in arousing fear in the child." Father is likely to be seen as the more powerful. There is some evidence for "mother preference," presumably due to her "nurturant" functions, and the "warm and satisfying connotations" of those functions.[14]

In a society as large and as internally differentiated as that of the United States, there are of course numerous regional, ethnic, and social class subcultures. It is to be expected that parental roles will vary between these subcultures, and childrens' perceptions along with them. Bernard C. Rosen examined child perceptions of parents, collecting questionnaire responses from 367 middle- and lower-class boys, ages nine through eleven. He concluded:

... boys from the middle-class tend to perceive their parents as more competent, emotionally secure, accepting and interested in their child's performance than do lower-class boys. Social class differences in the boy's perception of the parent were much greater with respect to the father than the mother.[15]

Parental roles, and children's parent perceptions, are distinctive in each of the many cultures markedly unlike United States culture or any of its subcultures.

There is for example a New Zealand Maori community in which "The mother has a considerably closer relationship with her middle-years children than does the father." The result, however, is not that her children feel especially warm toward her. Rather, "she is consequently the chief authority figure; it is nearly always 'Mum' who does the punishing." Father seldom concerns himself with discipline, but he "occasionally provides special threats, . . ." especially for his sons. Mother winds up on the short end of the stick; of the 52 children queried, only 20 per cent of boys and 35 per cent of girls prefer mother to father. In fact, there appears to be in this community an unusual lack of warmth as between parents and children. The psychologist who made the study regards these Maori as somewhat indifferent to their middle-years children, wanting from them mainly work and behavior of such a sort that they are not "nuisances" to their parents. It is reported that "the parents are most often seen [by the child] as either indifferent [toward him] . . . or else they may be directly or indirectly rejecting."[16]

A still more strained parent-child relationship is reported by J. Henry from the Pilaga Indians of the Argentine Gran Chaco. Among these people interpersonal relations generally tend to be strained and hostile; parent-child and child-sibling relations as well are apparently of the same order. Henry says:

. . . feelings of hostility toward parents and siblings are intense. . . . [The] behavior of the children is characterized by destructive attempts against the parents and siblings, by attempts as restitution, and by regression.[17]

This is the prevailing child-toward-parent pattern; the little children no doubt learn it from older ones, and the parents expect and accept it. The whole sociocultural system, including the prevalent indifference of parents, seems to be conducive to mistrust and jealousy.

. . . without status and deprived of warmth, the Pilaga child remains a poor hostile little flounderer for a number of years until he at last begins to take his place in the adult economic activity. [18]

Between the Maori and Pilaga modes of child perception and the prevalent mode in Thailand there is a striking difference. A young Thai woman explains (in unaccustomed English, and for the benefit of Americans) how children in her country perceive their parents:

The most respected persons in all Thai families are the parents. In children's groups the major cause of fighting is calling each other's parents bad names. I remembered that when I was in the fourth year of the primary school I had fought with a friend who was much, much bigger than me because she called my mother bad names and I never talked to her again until we had finished from school.[19]

The Thai king, she adds, is like "all the parents gathered together," and placed "high up, . . . and from there he will watch and take care of us," as parents watch over and care for their children.[20]

Navaho Indian children express strong and deep family attachments. They say they are "happy when the family is doing things together or when relatives visit, but they recall as sad occasions times when family members go away or are removed by death."[21] White children are about equally inclined toward pleasant associations with family and its activities, but they seem to be less affected by loss of family members. For Navaho children it is primarily the same-sex

53

parent who is associated with experiences of a happy sort, and with praise. "Persons beyond the limits of the family are felt to be something of a threat."[22]

Race and Ethnic Differentiations and Attitudes in the Culture of Middle Childhood

In our earlier discussion of race awareness in young children we reviewed studies showing that awareness begins in some children at three years, and in many by four. We have seen too how race attitudes develop in accord with prevalent cultural patterning. Middle-years children are of course almost sure to be even more aware, their attitudes even more clear cut. Vaughan, who has conducted numerous studies of Maori and of white children (ages four to twelve) in New Zealand, concludes: "American findings that ethnic awareness among both majority and minority group members increases with age are supported" by his research.[23]

Evidence concerning race awareness and attitudes comes also from a number of other studies. An important recent source is the work of psychiatrist Robert Coles. Dr. Coles has observed closely and sensitively many of the Negro and white children caught up in early phases of school integration in the South. Coles says:

Every Negro child I know has had to take notice in some way of what skin color signifies in our society. If they do not easily—or at all—talk about it, their drawings surely indicate that the subject is on their minds. . .

Negro children of elementary school age have not had enough time to set themselves straight about "why" they are colored and what that fact will mean for them in the future. Often they will tend to deny the fact, or they will accept it so extravagantly that it is clear they are yet confused and troubled. Ruby abstained from browns and blacks [in drawings]; another girl of six I knew in New Orleans could scarcely use any other color.[24]

A seven-year-old Negro boy, who found himself "alone in a white school" in North Carolina, drew for Coles a "rather robust white boy near the summit of a mountain, and a rather fragile Negro one well below." At Coles' invitation he explained his picture:

"Freddie [the Negro boy in the picture] wishes he were up top, like Billy [white], but he isn't, because there's not room for both of them up there, at least not now there isn't. . . . Freddie would be afraid to be on top. He wouldn't know what to do. He's used to where he is, just like Billy is."

Coles asked why Freddie was small. The child said:

"Freddie doesn't get to be so big, because he stoops over. He picks the crops and plows, so his back is bent. . . . But Billy, he can stretch when he wants to, and the air up there on top is real healthy for him. When they [Freddie and Billy] talk it's real hard, because they are far from one another, so they have to shout."[25]

A white classmate (also seven years old) said of the lone Negro child in his room: "Johnnie, he's not making any trouble, but he's different from the rest of us, and that's important. So he shouldn't be with us. . . ."[26] And then the white child drew and explained a picture. In it he represented the "color line" by a busy highway with whites and attractive buildings on one side, Negroes and an inferior setting on the other. He showed in his picture a bright red stop light. "No," he said when Coles asked if there was a green light sometimes; *"it's a big highway and you're not supposed to cross over"*[27]

Drawings collected by Wayne Dennis provide evidence that Negro children, unlike Caucasoid and Mongoloid children, admire other-race physical attributes.

. . . When children of the white race, whether from North America, Europe, or the Middle East, are asked to draw a man, almost all their drawings represent a white man . . . they almost never draw a Negro; of . . . 1650 white children . . . only one, a German boy, drew a Negro. [28]

Nor do Caucasian children draw "Asiatics," except rarely. On the other hand most Asiatics, insofar as their drawings are racially identifiable, do draw Asiatics. This inclination to draw own-race figures does not, however, extend to Negro children. They usually do not draw Negroes. Even among Sudanese Negroes the majority draw white men, and American Negro children very seldom draw a Negro. "The inescapable conclusion appears to be that Negro children who draw a white man are drawing the appearance which they would like to possess. . . . . Whatever their own race, the children draw men who have the physical features which they admire."[29]

An admiration of the physical features of whites, or of non-blacks, at any rate, is discoverable in social settings that might seem unlikely.

Where whites are relatively wealthy and influential it is not surprising if their physical appearance becomes the generally accepted standard. But it is more remarkable to find that in precolonial times native Africans, some of them at least, looked with special favor on peoples of relative lightness. In her autobiography Baba, an elderly Negro woman of the Muslim Hausa, recalls the Fulani people who came to her village when she was "a maiden." These Fulani were, she says, "light people with reddish skins." And she adds: "They weren't like Mai Sudan's people—those were Gwari, very black—these [Fulani] were beautiful people."[30] Perhaps Baba applies retrospectively standards she has learned since contact with Europeans. But there is reason to believe that her judgment reflects an indigenous standard. The Fulani were precolonial aristocrats who treated Baba's people with disdain, called them "commoner," and ordered them about. In the indigenous system of intertribal relations the "light people with reddish skins" had made themselves superordinate. Even among the Hausa color distinctions may have been made. Baba says of her mother, who died young, that "She was a beautiful woman with lovely hair and light skin."[31]

Negro children in contemporary South Africa give evidence of being preoccupied with race and race differences and of favoring whiteness. These are the findings in the Lambert and Klinesberg study of six-, ten-, and fourteen-year-olds in eleven nations.[32] Moreover, the views of Bantu children interviewed in this study are distinctive as compared with views of children in the other national groups.

Ethnic references played a prominent role in the thinking of only one group, the Bantu children, the only Negro group included in our study. Clearly race is of major social significance in South Africa and it is not surprising that it manifested itself in the thinking of those South Africans who are discriminated against because of their skin color.[33]

Own-group concepts and attitudes are found by Lambert and Klineberg to be predominantly favorable—and strongly so, for most groups—among American, Brazilian, English- and French-Canadian, French, German, Israeli, Lebanese, and Turkish children. Only Bantu and Japanese are omitted from this list; the former because they "gave few evaluative descriptions [of own group], instead of typically making references to similarities or referring to physical characteristics. . . ." The latter (Japanese children) are omitted because they "saw the Japanese as poor, intelligent, and bad . . . ."[34] It is reasonable to assume that the Japanese child's negative evaluations of own-group reflect a post-World War II wave of national self-assessment and self-criticism (these children were interviewed in 1959). The Bantu child perhaps reflects, in his disinclination to evaluate own-group, what has been observed in young Negro children in the United States—a tendency to avoid discussion of discomforting perceptions about the physical attributes and the social status of self and of other Negroes. Except for the Bantu and Japa-

56

nese, the children typically see his own kind as "good, wealthy, and free" (American); "good, intelligent, cultured, happy, and unambitious" (Brazilian); as "good, wealthy, peaceful, and patriotic" (French-Canadian); as "good, peaceful, religious, intelligent, and ambitious" (Israeli); and so forth.

There are exceptions, but on the whole children's views of their own group tend to be held also by the children of other groups; for example: "the American children's views of their own people generally agreed with other groups' views of Americans—that Americans are good, wealthy, and politically democratic...." But non-American children often add negative traits. "Likewise, the German children saw themselves as good, ambitious, wealthy, and intelligent, whereas many other groups of children, while agreeing that Germans are good, also saw them as aggressive and bad."[35] There are other cases, the Brazilian children, for example, whose concepts of their own groups are not matched outside it because the group is scarcely known, one way or another, to children of other groups.

All the children interviewed were asked what nationality or nationalities they would like to be, and not like to be, if they were free to choose. "... American nationality is the first choice for nine of the eleven groups of children, and, in general, its popularity increases at each successive age level." British and French are next most popular. "... Many groups of children say they would least like to be Russian, African, Chinese, or German, listed here in order of nomination."[36] The reasons given for both positive and negative choices have to do especially with what the children believe to be the characteristics of the people of the various countries (good or bad, intelligent or unintelligent) and with the conditions of life (wealthy or poor, clean or dirty). In all eleven groups there is considerable emphasis on the importance of aggressiveness or badness. Unintelligence was important especially for the Bantu, French, and Israeli children, and dirtiness was emphasized only by the Japanese and Bantu children. "These themes apparently reflect underlying cultural values that may be essential in shaping children's reactions to foreign peoples and nations."[37]

The children were asked to express their views about each of seven peoples: Americans, Brazilians, Chinese, Germans, Indians (India), African Negroes, and Russians. It appears that they tend to see Americans as most like themselves, and Chinese, Indians, and African Negroes as not like themselves. About Brazilians, the opinions of Germans and Russians with respect to similarities and differences tend to be divided within the national groups. On the whole, however, the researchers regard the responses as showing "an unex-

57

pectedly large amount of agreement in views about these seven peoples."[38] And they are impressed with the facts that the children often seem to associate with other peoples qualities and circumstances both favorable and unfavorable.

Americans, though seen primarily in positive terms (good, wealthy, and intelligent) are also seen as aggressive. Germans and Russians too are believed to be intelligent. Germans, Russians, Chinese, and African Negroes are sometimes characterized as aggressive. These four groups, in addition, are not infrequently labeled "bad." Indians, African Negroes, and Chinese are likely to be seen as poor. All seven peoples are regarded by significant numbers of children as being good. Only African Negroes are believed to be unintelligent and uncultured.

As might be expected, there is evidence of some boy/girl and some social class opinion differences within each national group. The more significant differences, however, are a matter of age. Opinions expressed by older children are on average richer in general content and richer in abstractions.

The descriptions of the younger children focussed on physical features, clothing, language, and habits in contrast to the older children's preoccupation with personality traits, habits, politics, religion, and material possessions . . . . Children apparently come to think about foreign peoples in an increasingly more stereotyped manner between six and fourteen years.[39]

However, Lambert and Klineberg conclude also:

. . . Six-year-olds characteristically viewed foreign peoples as different much more frequently than did ten-year-olds, who generally considered a much larger array of foreign peoples as similar [to own-group]. There was little change in similarity outlooks between ten and fourteen. . . . Six-year-olds . . . were least prone to express affection for foreign peoples, whether these were thought of as similar or dissimilar. In contrast, [children of] the ten-year age period . . . were particularly ready to view foreign peoples as similar and were especially friendly toward them, even those viewed as dissimilar. . . . It seems very likely that ignorance contributes to the suspicion or even fear of the strange noted at the six-year level. The fourteen-year-olds in general showed less openness and friendliness; . . . the favorable orientation noted at age ten did not hold up into the teen years.[40]

But these generalizations about age and child's-eye views admit of exceptions. The authors recognize that cultural factors can override age differences. Among the American, French-Canadian, and

Japanese children it is the fourteen-year-olds, more than the ten-year-olds, who exhibit friendly or affectionate out-group attitudes. Americans and Japanese, at age fourteen, appear to be conspicuously less prejudiced and ethnocentric than children of other ages or groups. Lambert and Klineberg regard their supporting evidence on this point as tenuous, however. Age distinctions aside, and the whole of their evidence considered, they conclude that American, French, English-Canadian, and French-Canadian children are comparatively friendly toward foreign groups. They find Japanese, Brazilian, Turkish, and Israeli children "more unfriendly."[41]

In their brief summary of massive data Lambert and Klineberg, of course, cannot answer all questions likely to arise in the minds of interested readers, nor could they have gathered all the evidence for which such questions might call. No one study, however extensive and careful, can achieve more than certain necessarily limited objectives. In this instance 300 children in each of eleven national groups were interviewed. In the United States this sample was drawn from a New England community, and we may suppose that samples drawn from other regions might have produced views of a somewhat different sort. One wonders too about the views of New England children, and children in other U.S. regions, toward people closer at hand than the foreign types on which the Lambert-Klineberg study focused.

In the Southwestern United States, most children probably develop by age six some concepts of Mexican-Americans, who are likely to have for "Anglo" children an aura of strangeness. In his "Confessions of an Anglo," native Southwesterner Maurice Schmidt opens a window on the child's-eye view as he recalls his own early impressions. Schmidt writes:

They are little, they are many, they always move in bunches, they are dark, talk fast until I come near and then stare with a mixture of suspicion and muteness. This is the first recollection I have of the Mexican-American, the first time I saw him, recognized him as someone different from myself. It was my first year in grammar school and the first year they were "allowed" to come to our school.[42]

"They" were widely believed to carry, somehow concealed in ragged clothing, "vicious pocket knives," and to be ready and able to use them. It was therefore dangerous to fight them, yet fights were commonplace. And, Schmidt adds:

Even though the little dark ones were supposed to be vicious, it was always the Anglo kids who provoked fights, who shouted "Spic" and "dirty Meskin." If the Mexican-American won the fight, he was punished. He was spanked in the principal's or teacher's office, more often and more viciously than was the Anglo. . . . [but] they never cry. . . .

My feelings towards them at first were a mixture of fear and curiosity. Later a different element began to enter.[43]

The new element was envy—envy of the "freedoms" the Mexican-American children enjoyed, and of what this Anglo child saw as a more exciting, even exotic, way of life. "They" were allowed to eat between meals and to go barefoot in the rain. "All good things were permitted them," and they had other advantages. Their houses and yards were more lively, noisy, and interesting; their grown-ups knew how to do things—how to build and plant and take care of tools.

Some years later, young Schmidt had learned to fight with his fists and to respect other boys who were good at it. He was a leader, and he instituted a new pattern.

The idea of outcasts, class distinctions, and snobbery even at that time repelled me. I made innovations in gangland. . . . I approached the Mexican-American gang and told them we ought to play together. They agreed to join us. To cement the new relationship I appointed one of them second only to myself in rank and gave him the additional honor of being my personal bodyguard.[44]

Schmidt grew up in a small town during a period of rapid change. The conservative townfolk resisted the change and blamed it on Roosevelt, but the Schmidts were a "Roosevelt family." Their son must have been well ahead of his peers in his acceptance of "Meskins," and his view of them was no doubt unusual. It would be less unusual today, though not necessarily the predominant view.

Where the predominant view is separatist on one or both sides of the ethnic or racial line, even "Roosevelt family" types, tolerant and independent thinkers, must find it difficult really to erase the line. Mark Twain makes the point, telling of his own Missouri farm childhood, and his relations with the Negro children he knew: "We were comrades, and yet not comrades; color and condition interposed a subtle line which both parties were conscious of and which rendered complete fusion impossible."[45]

Unselfconscious and deep friendships across racial lines are probably still most unusual in a United States now so radically changed in many ways. School integration has narrowed the physical distance between the races much more than the social distance.

60

Awareness of race difference remains sharp on both sides of the line, and hostilities are now freely expressed by Negro children as they are, and long have been, expressed by whites.

A study made in Houston, Texas (by Alma Beman and M. E. Goodman) provides some illustrative items.[46] Children of first through sixth grades, living in three poverty pockets of the city (one predominantly Negro, one Mexican-American, one Anglo) were interviewed in their homes. The interviews were lengthy. They were designed to elicit the child's views on his life at home, in his neighborhood, and in school, and his perceptions of the people he encounters in all these contexts.

Many of these children attend "mixed" schools. Among Anglo children especially, awareness of differences as well as own-kind preferences are evident. Of the 43 Anglo children interviewed, half mention color spontaneously when asked "What kind of kids are there at your school?" Nearly all the Anglos specify "white kids" when asked "What kinds of kids are best?" Neither Mexican-American nor Negro children spontaneously identify classmates in ethnic terms, and very few specify "best kids" in these terms. Prejudices are sometimes expressed forthrightly:

> The colored are best, 'cause I don't like bright people. (Negro boy, age 8)
> The white kids are best, 'cause the others are mean. (Anglo girl, age 9)
> We'll kick niggers out. (Anglo girl, age 10)
> There are Niggers and Mexicans and Bolidos at school. The Mexicans are best. (Mexican-American girl, age 9)

However, unconventional views are sometimes expressed:

> Ones that mind their own business [are best]. (Anglo girl, age 10)
> I play with all of them, even Negroes. I don't care what kind they are. (Anglo girl, age 9)
> Colored boys are best. (Anglo brothers, 9 and 10)
> Colored kids are best. (Mexican-American boy, age 8)

What then can we conclude about the concept of self and of others in the middle years of childhood? Aspirations for the self become increasingly salient, along with awareness of and concern for the image of the self among those others who are significant to the child.

There are, for example, distinct cultural differences. In traditional cultures, patterns reflecting the superordination/subordination axis of child-adult relations are ordinarily salient, and strongly so. But however clear cut the cultural patterning, there are in all societies some discrepancies between prescribed (ideal) and actual patterns of behavior. The discrepancies reflect individuality and ambivalence—feelings of both affection/gratitude and of hostility toward elders.

Children who are heir to cultures in which parent-child relationships are structured quite differently perceive the modal patterns of their worlds and structure their expectations accordingly.

The culture of the middle years also shows marked expansion of interest in own-kind/other-kind peoples and of stereotypes about their attributes and differences. Many studies provide evidence that children of racial and ethnic minorities, in the United States and elsewhere, are particularly aware of such differences and appreciative of the attributes (physical attributes particularly) of the majority groups.

NOTES

1. Hamed Ammar, *Growing Up in an Egyptian Village* (London: Routledge and Kegan Paul, 1954), p. 133.

2. Oscar Lewis, *La Vida* (New York: Random House, 1966) p. 246.

3. Norbert Wiener, *Ex-Prodigy* (Cambridge, Mass.: The Massachusetts Institute of Technology Press, 1964), p. 117.

4. Wallace E. Lambert and Otto Klineberg, *Children's Views of Foreign Peoples* (New York: Appleton-Century-Crofts, 1967), p. 89.

5. *Ibid.*, p. 90.

6. *Ibid.*, p. 96.

7. Grace Hechinger and Fred M. Hechinger, *Teen-Age Tyranny* (New York: William Morrow & Co., 1963).

8. Ammar, *op. cit.*, p. 129.

9. *Ibid.*, p. 131.

10. *Ibid.*, pp. 131 f.

11. Meyer Fortes, "Parenthood in Primitive Society," *Man*, 51 (1951), 65.

12. Bronislaw Malinowski, *Sex and Repression in Savage Society* (New York: Meridian, 1955 edition); Dorothy Eggan, "The General Problem of Hopi Adjustment," in Clyde Kluckhohn and Henry A. Murray, eds., *Personality in Nature, Society, and Culture* (New York: Alfred A. Knopf, 1948), pp. 220-235.

13. Anne Parsons, "Is the Oedipus Complex Universal?" in Robert Hunt, ed., *Personalities and Culture* (New York: Natural History Press, 1967), pp. 352-399.

14. Robert Dubin and Elizabeth Ruth Dubin, "Children's Social Perceptions: A Review of Research," *Child Development*, 36 (1965), 819 ff.

15. Bernard C. Rosen, "Social Class and the Child's Perception of the Parent," *Child Development*, 35 (1964), 1147.

16. Margaret Jane Earle, *Rakau Children* (Wellington, N. Z.: Victoria University, 1962), p. 60.

17. Jules Henry, "Some Cultural Determinants of Hostility in Pilaga Indian Children," *American Journal of Orthopsychiatry*, 10 (1940), 119.

18. *Ibid.*, p. 119.

19. Cornell University Southeast Asia Program, "A Simple One; The Story of a Siamese Girlhood," mimeographed (Ithaca, N.Y.: Cornell University, 1958), p. 30.

20. *Ibid.*, p. 30.

21. Dorothea Leighton and Clyde Kluckhohn, *Children of the People* (Cambridge, Mass.: Harvard University Press, 1947), p. 165.

22. *Ibid.*, p. 173.

63

[23]Graham M. Vaughan, "Ethnic Awareness in Relation to Minority Group Membership," *The Journal of Genetic Psychology*, 105 (1964), 128.

[24]Robert Coles, *Children of Crisis* (Boston: Little, Brown and Co., 1967), p. 62.

[25]*Ibid.*, pp. 67 f.

[26]*Ibid.*, p. 69.

[27]*Ibid.*, p. 70 (italics original).

[28]Wayne Dennis, *Group Values Through Children's Drawings* (New York: John Wiley and Sons, 1966), p. 67.

[29]*Ibid.*, pp. 74 f.

[30]M. F. Smith, *Baba of Karo, A Woman of the Muslim Hausa* (New York: Philosophical Library, 1955), p. 66.

[31]*Ibid.*, p. 75.

[32]Lambert and Klineberg, *op. cit.*, pp. 35 ff.

[33]*Ibid.*, p. 201.

[34]*Ibid.*, pp. 202 f.

[35]*Ibid.*, p. 203.

[36]*Ibid.*, pp. 207 f.

[37]*Ibid.*, p. 208.

[38]*Ibid.*, p. 209.

[39]*Ibid.*, pp. 211 f.

[40]*Ibid.*, pp. 216 f.

[41]*Ibid.*, p. 219.

[42]Maurice Schmidt, "Confessions of an Anglo," *The Texas Observer* 31 March 1967, p. 14.

[43]*Ibid.*, p. 14.

[44]*Ibid.*, p. 15.

[45]Mark Twain (Samuel L. Clemens), *Mark Twain's Autobiography* (New York: (Harper and Brothers, 1924), I, 100.

[46] Alma Beman and Mary Ellen Goodman, "Child's-Eye-Views of Life in an Urban Barrio," mimeographed (Houston: Rice University Center for Research in Social Change and Economic Development, 1968), *passim.*

5

Self and Others:
Responsibilities,
Relationships, and Roles

... What is there more offensive, more
unsuitable, than the sight of a sulky or
imperious child, who commands those
about him, and impudently assumes the
tones of a master toward those without
whom he would perish?

Jean-Jacques Rousseau

No aspect of the culture of childhood has greater practical significance than its patternings in matters having to do with what may be
called "citizenship."

For children, as for adults, being a "citizen"—a member of society—involves knowing what is expected in one's society and being
in command of relevant skills—knowing how to do what is expected.
What are one's work and social obligations and responsibilities? To
whom is one accountable—who are the authorities of one's world,
and how is each likely to exert his authority? What is regarded as
good, bad, or ethically neutral? To what extent are the standards and
the authorities flexible?

Being a "citizen" involves not only knowing about but also caring
about what is expected. It is a matter of feelings, and of sentiments, as well as of knowledge. This "caring about" is the realm of
internalized standards—of values and conscience (which we will
examine more closely in Chapter 6). The controls exercised by society
become for most individuals, children included, a matter of what

has been learned—truly internalized—as well as a matter of what is imposed from without by enforcement of rule and law.

What a child of three or four or five will know or care about responsibilities and relationships is highly variable between societies. And in all societies, even the very small and close-knit, it will vary widely between individual children. But here we must continue to talk, as we have before, mainly in terms of what appear to be the usual—the modal—types. We cite particular individual cases or selected small groups mainly when we have reason to regard them as usual in their time and society or subsociety, and therefore illustrative of the prevailing lifeways of children in that time and place.

Work and Defense: Early Childhood Obligations and Responsibilities

In the large majority of small and nonliterate societies, even in peasant societies, children early assume serious obligations and responsibilities. This is not to say that there are no differences; in some such societies children are not expected to do real work until they are six or older. But in such societies much more is likely to be expected of children under six than in most of the modern urban-industrial societies. In the matter of minimal expectations, modern American middle-class city people have probably no peers in all the world. They may expect developmental precocity, or at least rejoice in it—in early speaking, walking, evidence of talent, or intelligence, for example —but this is quite unlike an expectation of work and the assumption of real responsibilities.

It is true that the modern urban milieu provides little in the way of opportunities for real work by children. It is true too that in this modern milieu childhood is regarded as a period of training for adult responsibilities, and children are therefore expected to take seriously the opportunities and responsibilities of training. Permissiveness is commonplace in the more affluent modern settings, however, and adults are inclined to worry about overly heavy "pressures" on children. In traditional societies, by contrast, adults are unlikely to suffer from such concerns. On the contrary, they assume the validity of patterned expectations, and worry when children fail to meet those expectations. The expectations are not subject to question; the children who fail to meet them are. In the affluent American suburbs the situation is exactly reversed.

Anthropological literature is full of evidence that even young children can be competent with respect to subsistence technology and defense as well, and that their competence may serve them as a source of great pleasure and pride.

A Cheyenne Indian boy was given a little bow and some arrows as soon as he could run about. Thereafter "much of his time was spent in practice with the bow"; he shot at targets and at birds and other small creatures. "Little boys eight or ten years of age killed numbers of small birds with their arrows, and sometimes even killed them on the wing."

Though he keenly enjoyed the pursuit, the Cheyenne boy did not hunt merely for pleasure. To him it was serious work. He was encouraged to hunt by his parents and relatives, and was told that he must try hard to be a good hunter, so that hereafter he might be able to furnish food for the lodge, and might help to support his mother and sisters. . . . In their hunting . . . [the boys] displayed immense caution and patience. . . .

While engaged in hunting . . . they came to understand the signs of the prairie, to know the habits of wild animals, learned how to observe, how to become trackers, where the different birds and animals were found, and how they acted under different conditions; and were training themselves to habits of endurance and patience.[1]

Before he was nine, Black Elk, who was to become a great man among the Sioux, "was riding horses and could shoot prairie chickens and rabbits" with his bow. This was expected, and it was expected too that from the age of five or six all the boys would make a game of playing war. Black Elk says, in his autobiography:

The boys of my people began very young to learn the ways of men, and no one taught us; we just learned by doing what we saw, and we were warriors at a time when boys now are like girls. . . . I was thirteen years old and not very big for my age . . . [when my aunt gave me a six-shooter] and told me I was a man now. . . . We boys had practiced endurance, and . . . I could shoot straight with either a bow or a gun.[2]

Shortly thereafter Black Elk rode with the men in an attack on a cavalry unit of *Wasichus* (white men). Like the full-grown warriors he rode hanging low on his pony on the side away from the enemy, while shooting under the pony's neck. "This was not easy to do," he recalls, "even when your legs were long, and mine were not yet very long."[3]

In prerevolutionary Mexico poor peasant boys were likely to be put to work at six or seven looking after the oxen and carrying water. Pedro Martinez recalls that his uncle, for whom he worked at age seven, "didn't give me one moment to play. . . . I even forgot how to play marbles." His uncle did, however, give him time for a daily reading lesson, after which he was not infrequently whipped for a poor performance. "And that's the way it went, day in and day out for a whole year. My sister was no better off, she worked very hard."[4] At age ten Pedro was hired out as a regular *hacienda* laborer; he was one of a work gang of eighty little boys. "By the time I was twelve years old," he says, "I was working all the time."[5]

In tribal life, girls too have responsibilities important to the welfare of the group. A Hausa woman of Nigeria recalls:

When the midday food was ready, the women of the compound would give us children the food, one of us drew water, and off we went to the farm to take the men their food at the foot of a tree; I was about eight or nine at that time, I think. [probably ten to eleven years old, says M. G. Smith in notes accompanying the autobiography].[6]

From the age of nine or ten Klamath Indian girls learned to dry huckleberries, to dig and bake certain roots, gather and to grind "wokas" (a seed which was a staple of the diet), and to make mats, baskets, and clothing. An elderly Klamath woman describes her childhood experiences in learning these techniques:

[To dry huckleberries] you have to watch the fire for a day and a night. . . . [For baking camas—roots] you have to make the rocks hot just like for a sweat bath and put them in the pit with wet grass over them so the camas will steam. . . . I kept asking my mother how to do it, and she told me. . . . It was hard. . . .[7]

From the Middle Ages to the seventeenth century children in Europe "were weaned late, but then went very directly, at about the age of seven or eight, into the world of adults." In that world they were expected to assume responsibility, and to share "in the tasks and play of the community."[8]

The East African Chaga, a people whose economy depends upon cattle and agriculture, provide another instance of early and cheerful assumption of work roles by children. Boys and girls work at the same tasks—girls' tasks—until the boys are six or a little older. Thereafter the boys turn to participation in man's work and association mainly with boys and men. But as soon as they can toddle, children are at work looking after smaller babies, carrying water or firewood, helping to prepare food, cleaning animal quarters, "sweeping the yard, cutting fodder, and thatching the house." Both sexes enjoy this work, we are told, but "girls are better workers than boys,

. . . more painstaking, and less inclined to neglect their charges, or to steal their food."⁹

The labor of Chaga children, even in their early years, is highly valued by their parents and grandparents. By ancient custom the latter may claim a child as their own (first child to the paternal, and second to the maternal grandparents). The claim is not always exercised, and "often the transfer does not take place until a definite need for [the child's] help arises—for instance, if the grandmother is widowed."

The custom has sentimental and status justifications as well as practical aspects. The wealth and status of grandparents are in part measured by the number of grandchildren living with them and working for them. The Chaga explain:

"You Europeans can pay wages for a 'boy.' We can't afford that. Therefore our children are given to our parents to work for them." . . . A poor man's ambition is to have at least two grandchildren with him—a boy to pasture his cattle, a girl to cut fodder and clean the dung from the hut.¹⁰

Work skills become, quite obviously, a part of the culture of early childhood. Those work skills require early achievement of certain motor skills as well as appropriate knowledge and attitudes. In his study of Chaga children Raum describes in detail some of the spontaneous physical exertions of a little boy from ten months to one year and two months. During this time the boy learned to walk with excellent balance and to coordinate skillfully hand, foot, leg, arm, and body movements. There followed a period of avid play with sticks and then, from seventeen months, with garden hoes. The child soon began to help his mother and elder siblings with the weeding, and "at two years and three months he had made a little irregular garden for himself without advice or control from any of his elders."¹¹ Raum comments on the universality of certain of these experiments and learnings, and on the cultural uniqueness of certain others. He says:

These activities [learning to walk and coordinate] are common to healthy children all over the world . . . [but there can be seen here] a fixation of certain movements which do not receive such emphasis in other cultures. A definite bias in the cultural milieu of the Chaga child tends to canalize his motor energies in one direction, such as the handling of stick, spoon, and knife, and to perfect the co-ordination of movements useful for it.¹²

Chaga women carry loads of grass and firewood balanced expertly on their heads. Raum recorded the successive steps through which a little girl spontaneously practiced this skill, beginning before she was one year old. By the age of three she was "an accomplished mother's help."[13]

Among the Cheyenne Indians of the American Great Plains, the early motor skills of girls were much like those of the Chaga, but this similarity did not hold for boys. Cheyenne women carried firewood on their backs. At age three or four a little girl "might be seen marching proudly along" beside her mother, carrying "a backload of slender twigs" while her mother "staggered under a heavy burden of stout twigs."[14] The Cheyenne, like the Sioux, were great horsemen, and riding skills were a part of the child's early repertoire. Grinnell reports:

Boys learned to ride almost as soon as they learned to walk. From earliest babyhood infants were familiar with horses and their motions, and children two or three years of age often rode in front of or behind their mothers, clinging to them or to the horses' manes. They thus gained confidence, learned balance, and became riders. . . . By the time they were five or six years of age, the boys were riding young colts bareback. Soon after this they began to go into the hills to herd the ponies. They early became expert in the use of the rope for catching horses.[15]

Social Obligations and Responsibilities

In societies like these, and in many complex societies as well, the culture of early childhood includes the skills and knowledge necessary to meet social as well as work obligations and responsibilities. Proper behavior in the presence of elders is a prime obligation. Among the Cheyenne "the first lesson that the child learned was one of self-control—self-effacement in the presence of its elders." Crying babies were not tolerated in the lodge; their mothers carried them out if they could not be hushed. "If older people were talking, and a tiny child entered the lodge and began to talk to its mother, she held up her finger warningly, and it ceased to talk, or else whispered its wants to her."[16]

Little children of the Chippewa Indians were equally meticulous in the matter of social obligations. An adult recalls:

We were told not to look at any person a long time; nor to make fun of anyone, but to respect all people. We were told, too, to say "goodbye" or to look at people once more just before they left; that was a sign that they were welcome to come again. Children were often given tobacco and told to present it to older persons as a sign of good will and friendship . . . [children were taught] that they must not go peeking in the wigwams after dark and that they . . . must not go to the neighbors when they were eating and look wistfully at the food. Little children were taught not to go between older people and the fire. . . .[17]

Through these and numbers of other patterns the child was exhibiting a basic Chippewa value—kindness. "It was really not manners that were taught," says Hilger's informant; "it was more like kindness." Other relevant patterns were taught "by observation and participation." Hilger's informants told her:

A mother would put some food into a dish and tell her child to take it to the neighbors, and so teach the child to give and share. A mother seldom gave anything away herself; she always gave it to one of the children to give, so the child would grow up to give and be willing to give. . . . If a family had much meat because of a successful hunt, everybody was invited to come and get some, and the children saw this.[18]

A well-rounded philosophy of life was taught to young children, even drilled into them, in these and other American Indian societies. A Hopi man recalls his grandfather's instruction:

"My grandson, old people are important. They know a lot and don't lie. Listen to them, obey your parents, work hard, treat everyone right. Then people will say, 'That boy Chuka is a good child. Let's be kind to him.' . . . This is the trail that every good Hopi follows. . . ."

He advises me to keep bad thoughts out of my mind, to face the east, look to the bright side of life, and learn to show a shining face, even when unhappy. . . . He taught me to get up before sunrise, bathe and exercise my body, and look around for useful work to do. He said, "Work means life. No one loves a lazybones."[19]

In peasant villages social obligations of these sorts are generally taught and learned from infancy. In Tepotzlan, Mexico, the little child knows that obedience and unobtrusiveness—"good" behavior—toward his elders are expected. "Most children are subdued and inhibited in the presence of their father [especially] and remain so well into adulthood. They are less consistent in their behavior toward their mother. . . ."[20] In the French village of Peyrane the children are, to an American's eye, "incredibly well behaved. They are courteous, docile, gentle, cooperative, respectful; . . . they are gentle and patient with children younger than they. Above all they have a sense of dignity and social poise."[21]

In highly complex societies—those of China, Japan, and England, for example—the prevailing patterns were until recently much like the patterns of these peasant societies. Young children were objects of deep affection; they were sheltered, loved, and trained. But adults were in charge, and to them were owed both respect and obedience. These obligations were well understood and sharply etched among the patterns of the childhood cultures.

Citizenship Patterns in a Sample of American Four-Year-Olds

In modern American society, in its urban middle-class segment at any rate, the obligations of young children are few and of quite different sorts. With respect to work, or "chores," little is likely to be expected of the preschool child. We have been told by nursery school four-year-olds, whom we interviewed and observed extensively, that their mothers, fathers, and teachers ask them to put away or "pick up" toys or other things, to run small errands, and occasionally to help with the dishes. Beyond these less than heavy tasks nothing is asked or expected except that the child cooperate with respect to essential personal routines—especially eating, sleeping, toileting, dressing, and undressing. His major "obligation" is to play, to "have fun."[22]

These American four-year-olds know about certain social expectations having to do with social order and the welfare or safety of others (for example, you should "be quiet when someone else is asleep" or "when someone is talking," "do as you are asked," "share with your friends"). They are aware of certain limitations on personal freedom of choice and activity (for example: don't take food without permission, don't touch others' things). The actual behavior of these children, as reported by parents and teachers and as we observed it, conforms fairly well with expectations of which they are aware. Like most adults, they by no means match perfectly their behavior patterns with the ideal patterns of their culture.

However, discrepancies are frequent and striking in only a few of the 92 children we studied. These few are quite often defiant and resentful, aggressive and hostile, toward parents and teachers. It is these same children who most often spin fantasies involving the violent and morbid, and who exhibit a sophisticated and even cynical command of pretentious techniques. Rousseau's "sulky and imperious" child appears as a small minority in our sample of the four-year-old "citizens" of the urban middle class.

The majority of these four-year-olds readily admits that there are certain things they *have* to do, but a sizable minority rejects this notion. More numerous still are those who reject the notion that there are any things they must *not* do. In many cases, cultural pressure is not strongly perceived or is too ineffectual to require acknowledgement. Children in less permissively-oriented societies would be unlikely to assert a freedom from "thou shalt" and "thou shalt not."

With respect also to concepts of "must" and "must not" these children are unlike children growing up in the traditional societies. The "must" regulations that occur to these American boys and girls center upon the self and its functions—upon a private sphere. It is only among the prohibitions that a significant proportion recognizes adult mandates pertaining primarily to others—to a public sphere. If we read the implications correctly these children are learning to think negatively about this latter sphere; it is likely to be otherwise in societies more concerned with group welfare.

What these four-year-olds declare they "love" and "hate" to do is instructive and relevant also to the comparison with other societies. When asked about either of these matters there are few children who fail to turn their attention to the private sphere. Some notable exceptions to this generalization do occur, however, and it is significant that they occur particularly in the case records of those children whom we find to be especially responsive and positive with respect to social obligations. It is they who "love" to extend courtesies or to do things for other people.

It appears that the responses of children to standards in the home and to standards in the nursery school are not the same. Possibly this difference is more apparent than real; it may be a function of unlikeness in the standards themselves, of differences in severity of judgment, or of differences in the actual level of conformity at school and at home. Whatever the meaning, we find teachers somewhat more inclined than mothers to give children the benefit of any doubt as to whether standards are understood, and somewhat more inclined to assert that their expectations are met, and without prodding or urging.

Moreover, teachers, as compared with mothers, report a notably lower proportion of cases showing really "out-of-bounds" behavior. Checking these evaluations against recorded observations of actual behavior (in the school) lends support to the mothers. Perhaps it merely shows observers and mothers judging similarly, and both judging rather less tolerantly than teachers. There is, in any case, remarkable agreement between observers and mothers concerning the number of children given to out-of-bounds behavior, upon occasion at least. (Mothers report 41; our observation records show 42.)

As the children view the content of standards there is no vast difference between home and school. The authorities in both places are especially given to telling them to get on with the personal routines—the sleep or resting and so on, and with their picking up, putting away, or other chores. Parents, however, issue prohibitions about personal safety—on the street or about the car or the stove or with respect to inclement weather, while teachers' "don'ts" have to do especially with social safety—with "don't hit" and the like. On the whole these four-year-olds are quite aware of the things they are being told to do and not to do, and these things reflect an adult focus on establishing habits to ensure physical well-being and the assumption of responsibility for own behavior.

That the children also conceive of obligations as a reciprocal matter is attested by both adults and the children themselves. More than half the latter declare that there are things other people should do for them, and the specifics they list are much like the ones they accept as their own obligations.

Fewer children (about 40 per cent) respond affirmatively when asked about their negative obligations (what they should *not* do to others) and the reciprocal negative obligations of others. But the greatly predominant emphasis of the negative obligations they do conceive is "don't fight" (hit, kick, etc.).

To recognize obligations may be a quite different thing than to *feel* ready and even eager to act upon them. To *say* that one does may be also a different thing than to actually feel so. More than half of these children know the "right" answers in connection with their obligations to others. Perhaps they also know the "right" answers in connection with the way they should *feel* about acting on these obligations. Over half of all the children declare that there are one or more things (sharing, helping, and so forth) they *like* to do for others, while only a third admit to things they don't like to do for others. We can only assume that, for the most part, the children mean what they say. Apparently, in spite of the focus on self that is the human birthright and the American fetish, over half of these four-year-olds have already yielded in some degree to the countereffects of social give-and-take and to the altruistic-cooperative *mores* that also flourish in American culture.

We have noted earlier some sharp contrasts between children whose attitudes are highly positive and others who are highly negative. Their modes of relating to people are in sharp contrast. The pattern at the negative pole is marked by assertive, insistent, emotional, and unreasonable preoccupation with the child's own rights and the obligations of others toward them. The child is aggressive, hostile, uncritical of himself and highly critical of the interpersonal behavior of others. He is sometimes most candid in admitting to acceptance of some restraints; for example: "I would like to break their dishes and hurt them, but I don't." And he is sometimes candid in admitting to what he feels and fantasies; for example: "I hate somebody—I kill them."

The large majority of our four-year-olds give evidence that they are aware of that polarity so deeply built into American culture —the polarity of good and bad. Moreover, as mothers tell us, nearly all of the subjects are quick to judge what is good and what is not.

How do these children categorize people and behavior with respect to "good" and "bad"? Their mothers say, and the teachers agree within their admitted limits of knowledge, that it is matters of interpersonal relationship that the children most often judge as good or bad. Within the nature of interpersonal behavior they also conceive of interpersonal obligations as good when they share, help, play (nicely) with, are friendly, are kind, are polite, and so forth, and as good when others do these things. They see the opposite kinds of interpersonal relations as bad, and most often mention fighting, hitting, snatching, and so forth, as specifics. These findings reinforce our conclusion from the interpersonal relations data: *mores* of "civilized" social living have without doubt become a part of the life styles of more than half of these children.

But to be fair in judging good or bad and to be able to measure the self against the yardstick applied to others are quite sophisticated achievements. Parents and teachers agree that some 55 per cent of the 92 children do usually judge fairly, and that about half of them usually judge themselves much as they judge others. We should assume that the adults make these statements keeping in mind a level of expectation relative to age.

Child's-Eye Views of Adults: Their Relationships, Work, and Play

Judging others, whether peers or adults, seems to be a universal inclination among children. It is no doubt a part of the more general practice of watching one's fellows closely and critically. For children the practice is particularly instructive when guided by a lively curiosity.

"By the time I was seven and eight years of age, when I began to know things, I used to think about the children, large and small, and boys of different sizes up to a tall man." So says an elderly Navaho Indian. And he continues:

I used to look at children who were smaller than I was and think they were that size all the time, and I thought that I would be the same size always, and that men too were always that same size. I used to wish I were that tall. It worried me when I looked at myself and thought, "I'm a small boy. I won't grow up to be like these tall men."[23]

"Son of Old Man Hat" remembers too his curiosity about anatomical difference between boys and girls. He asked his mother about it. She chided him for saying "bad things," and added only that "girls are born that way, and you're a boy and born that way." But Hat's mother warned him: "You shouldn't bother the girls. It's bad for you." This warning was accompanied by some vivid misinformation about what girls and women could do to the male organ ("bite it off"). Students of Navaho culture (for example, Dorothea Leighton and Clyde Kluckhohn, 1947) report that the myth of the *vagina dentata* is well-known.[24] Hat continues:

So I began to be afraid and didn't dare go near them [girls] .... I thought about women too, and about babies. I'd look at a woman when she was pregnant and see that her belly was growing all the time.... I used to think about these babies and wonder where they got air, and how they breathed, while they were still inside the mother. I thought a whole lot about that....

I saw many a baby born at my place. When one was born I'd go close and see that the baby's stomach was full. I wondered how they ate and who'd been feeding them inside the mothers ... And about husband and wife ... I wondered how they were that way, and what kind of relatives they were to each other.[25]

Again he asked his mother, but her answers were of no help at all. She only assured him that his father was her husband, and she her husband's wife. One day Hat too would have a wife, and "when she wants to leave you ... you'll be hanging onto her, crying and begging her not to go, just as if she were your mother." The idea was preposterous! Hat was sure he would never, ever, go near a woman to whom he was not related.

When I was out herding and saw a billy-goat or a ram get on a goat or sheep I used to think, "A man must do just the same thing to a woman." ... When a man and a woman were around together I used to watch them closely, but I never saw a man get on a woman.[26]

Many a child, under tribal conditions of life particularly, does witness the "primal scene." And many more undoubtedly arrive at logical conclusions after witnessing copulation between domestic or wild animals.

76

In a one-room dwelling the "facts of life" are not very long a secret. Children also get a good deal of sex education through sheep herding, partly from watching the animals, partly from the opportunities which isolation offers for exhibitionism and experiment.[27]

We know remarkably little about these aspects of child thought and perception. Autobiographies are seldom so explicit about early speculations as is Hat's, and children's early questions and comments are seldom either encouraged or recorded. But many of us, if we were to state honestly and fully the memories of our own early curiosities and speculations, might tell stories similar to Hat's, and reaching back well before the age of seven or eight.

We might also tell, as Hat does, of childhood husband-and-wife play. One summer day he and a little girl were sent to keep the crows away from the ripening corn. Whiling away the time, these children "made a little brush hogan" (a house), and the little girl ground corn as though she were going to make cornbread, as wives do. And, Hat adds: "When she sat in this little brush hogan I'd be lying right close beside her, because, I thought, she's my wife and I'm her husband."[28]

Husband-wife relations of less intimate sorts are of interest, and sometimes profoundly impressive, to children. Violent quarrels observed or overheard may be remembered by a child through all his life. As Hat remembers, "One afternoon my father and mother began fighting." He describes in detail the "cussing," the hitting, wrestling, throwing down, and so on. He continues: "At last they stopped, they must have been tired, and just cussed each other." Hat's father then packed his things and made ready to leave, but at this point mother "was crying and begging him not to go."

They talked for a long time. Then he [father] put down his pack, and for a long time after that they talked. At last they all apologized to one another [mother, father, and father's second wife]. . . . Sometime after this my mother and father got into a quarrel again. . . .[29]

This time it was mother who threatened to leave, and did in fact leave, taking "her sheep and goats from my father's herd," riding her horse with Hat behind her. But the next morning, "she packed all the stuff on the horse again and said, 'We'll go back, my son, to your father.'" Another reconciliation followed.

As soon as we got inside she walked up to him and put her arms around his neck and held him against her breast. She was crying and talking, saying, "I'll be with you all the time. I'm not going to treat you like this any more. Forgive me, my husband." . . . She talked for a long time while she cried and held him.[30]

These episodes were due, as Hat understood it, to his mother's jealousy toward his father's second wife. A third fight developed when his father became jealous of a male visitor. He "whipped" the mother and declared he was leaving her. Again she cried and begged him to stay, and he did.

Hat remembers too the behavior of his parents before visitors. "They were always happy when anyone came, and they always joshed each other." Even his father's teasing his mother about her first husband provoked only a mild and humorous defense. That man, she said, was a good provider; he saved her from starvation. "He was good and kind. He was kind saving me for you." Mother added a ribald joke about what had been saved, and "they were all laughing about it."[31]

The detail and vividness of Hat's recollections, and his candor, are unusual. But what he experienced must surely be commonplace in nearly every society. Some psychologists assume that the witnessing of violent quarrels, like the witnessing of the "primal scene," must necessarily constitute trauma for the child, and very likely permanent psychological scars as well. There is in Hat's "dead-pan" account no hint of either trauma or scars.

The effects of such experiences must be highly variable from society to society, and closely related to culturally patterned expectations—to what is considered normal or tolerable in a given society or subsociety. Sex and violence are commonplace and taken-for-granted aspects of the round of life in many societies, or in certain segments of them. They are commonplace in the experience of the children of the big-city poor, as Oscar Lewis has shown to be the case in Mexico City, New York, and San Juan, Puerto Rico. Individual children vary greatly in ability to withstand the shocks and tensions to which they are exposed or in their phychic toughness and resiliency. And there may be compensatory experiences—of affection, for example—that help to make a positive balance of the impact of childhood observations and perceptions. This favorable balance may have prevailed in the case of Hat, who was loved, instructed, and cared for by both parents, by siblings, and by others as well. Hat remembers many instances of affection and solicitude. Of his elder sister, as she left the family hogan for a new home with her husband, he says:

I was on the hill, watching them go, and when I saw her turn around I started crying. I was so acquainted with her, and she treated me awfully kind. She was so kind to me. I thought of all those things, and that made me cry, until they went over the hill.[32]

Watching grownups must lead a child toward conclusions about the personalities and roles of men and women, about characteristic differences between them. His conclusions may be more or less representative of what is in fact modal in his society. They are likely to include much that is culturally patterned, as well as something that is distinctive to the individuals he happens to have observed.

Hat declares that as a child he "always thought a man was bigger and stronger." He thought:

A man is sensible, and knows more, and he's smarter than a woman. The man is way ahead, and the woman is way behind, because a man can do anything. A man can do all the hard work. . . . A woman can do certain work, but all she does is cook and work on blankets and herd sheep and carry water for a short distance and carry just an armful of wood.[33]

On the Navaho reservation, and in rural or tribal settings quite generally, children can see, imitate, and participate in the work done by their elders. But when subsistence work is removed from the vicinity of the home and when it becomes highly specialized, as in the modern city, children may know much less about it. Sociologists and psychologists have made a great deal of this difference, and no doubt it exists and has its effects on children and on parent-child relations. Yet the city child's ignorance of father's occupation can be overstated. One team of investigators reports "a correlation of 0.88 between the occupations of the fathers as described by 13-14 year olds and as given by the fathers themselves." Hilde Himmelweit and her research colleagues add, concerning urban lower- and middle-middle-class children in England:

. . . we found that even the dull 10-11 year olds were able to describe their father's job with sufficient detail. . . . Here are some examples of the children's responses: . . .
[1] An inspector of refrigerators. My father finds the dents and scratches in the doors and cabinets of refrigerators. If he finds a scratch he marks it with a crooked line, and a dent he marks with a circle. . . .
[2] Sorter in the Post Office. He sorts letters into one of 68 holes in a wooden frame. There are different frames for every town.
[3] At _____'s. He serves people with clothes. He is second to Head and could have been head of the shop.[34]

Whether or not he can describe his father's work, as did these English children, an urban child of the middle years will most likely be aware of many adult occupations and activities. He will think of many of them as appropriate to men or to women. Ruth E. Hartley has investigated "the development of [urban American, middle-class, nonminority] children's concepts of adults' sex-based social roles, with the major emphasis on women's roles." Her subjects were eight- and eleven-year-olds, about half of whom "had mothers who were employed at the time the children were interviewed or who had been employed for an appreciable length of time within the life-time of the child. . . ." Hartley says:

Those who have been concerned about a possible "confusion" on the part of children concerning male and female roles, because so many traditionally "feminine" and so many historically "masculine" tasks are now performed by members of both sexes, will be interested to know that on the basis of our data we can say with confidence that it is not *children* who are confused.[35]

The children are not confused, but they are conventional. Women sew and mend, wash, and shop. Men build and repair things, drive or operate vehicles, supervise or carry out factory or service operations, put out fires, and so forth. These typically are seen as female- and as male-type activities. Men are seen as sometimes doing venturesome things—climbing mountains, capturing wild animals—while women are thought to stay generally "close to home, serving, comforting, making small decisions and having coffee in the middle of the afternoon."[36]

There are, as the children see the matter, a good many activities in which both men and women take part (church-going, reading, travel). There are other activities assigned about as frequently to men as to women (teaching, working in such places as restaurants or nightclubs, visiting, helping children with homework).

Attitudes toward what adults might regard as "real work" tend toward the negative, a finding much like the "antiwork factor" reported in an earlier study. Hartley suggests this is to be expected; American children hear at home a good deal of parental grumbling about work. "Few children see the other side of the coin, the enduring gratification of working well at a congenial task . . ."[37]

This may be true. What is perhaps more important, American children are heavily exposed to such a "fun morality" as can hardly exist except in an affluent society or in the affluent and leisured segments of highly stratified societies.

Some further understanding of child awareness and attitudes with respect to the activities of grownups is to be found in my own comparative study of Japanese and American children of first through eighth grades.[38] The study involved approximately 1,250

Japanese (living in Central Honshu) and 3,750 American children (of the Northeastern United States), all urban or suburban, and largely middle-class families. Each child wrote for us a composition on the topic: "What I want to be when I grow up, and why."

A great variety of occupations are known to the children in both nations (see Tables 2 and 3).

Table 2. Occupational Choices of Japanese and American Boys

| | Japanese % | | American % | |
	Grades 1-4	Grades 5-8	Grades 1-4	Grades 5-8
Business	21.8	21.8	6.2	7.3
Professions	11.4	25.5	25.0	50.4
Military roles	—	—	8.5	6.7
Manual and related	27.5	14.5	26.3	8.2
Teaching	4.7	3.0	1.0	0.9
Religious roles	—	0.2	1.7	1.7
Specialties	13.3	11.0	6.7	7.5
Sports	12.8	10.8	16.3	9.2
Arts	2.4	6.1	3.5	5.3
Miscellaneous	6.2	7.0	4.9	2.8
Total	100.1	99.9	100.1	100.0
N	211	427	923	899

Japanese boys are highly aware of business activities, and much more interested in them than are American boys. Concepts of business roles differ too. In Japan the boys speak of the "company man" or "officer man," of the banker, the factory or store owner, the founder or employees of a "trading company." American boys speak most often of salesmen and merchandisers.

Among American boys, and older Japanese boys, there is high awareness of the professions, and great interest in them. To boys of both nations the doctor is by far the most conspicuous professional. The "scientist" and the "engineer" are often mentioned, and, in Japan, the "architect." The "lawyer" gets more attention from boys in the United States, the "professor" more from Japanese boys.

What we have classified as "specialties" includes a number of diverse occupations requiring considerable talent, training, or both. The specialty of major interest to the Japanese boys involves political activity and public office-holding. For the older American it is activities associated with the mass media, such as radio or TV announcing or news reporting. American boys, the younger ones especially, exhibit keen interest in flying—in the role of the pilot. Few Americans talk of the sea and the "ship captain," but a good many Japanese do so. Of rather minor interest in both countries is the pharmacist. The photographer is mentioned by small proportion of American boys, and by no Japanese.

Among national differences none is more striking than those having to do with military roles. These are entirely ignored by the Japanese, but not by the Americans, whose interest in the roles of the military pilot, the "officer," the soldier, sailor, or marine is not negligible.

It is important to note also that in connection with military role choices the Americans express much patriotic sentiment and much concern for the national safety; in fact, they do a great deal of verbal flag-waving. We got absolutely nothing of the sort from the Japanese boys.[39]

In the category "manual and related" occupations we include expression of interest in such skilled trades as carpenter, electrician, or mechanic. This category includes also transport workers (bus or cab drivers), police and firemen, farmers, ranchers, cowboys. Work of these sorts is quite prominent in the eyes of younger boys of both nations. Even among the older boys these activities are of considerable interest, especially in Japan.

Professional sports get attention at both age levels and in both countries. The large majority of sports-minded American boys and half of the Japanese boys specify baseball as the primary interest. In Japan a traditonal form of wrestling—*sumo*—competes with baseball for boys' attention.

No other occupational roles are of interest to significant numbers of the boys in either country. Teaching is of almost no interest to American boys and of interest to rather few in Japan, where teachers often are men. As we previously noted, military roles are ignored by the Japanese, who are indifferent to religious roles as well. The latter, though seldom mentioned by American boys, are of interest to some. The arts—drawing, acting, singing, or playing an instrument—are of more interest to older than to younger boys in both countries, but of no great interest to either.

With respect to the Japanese and American girls there are some notable and statistically significant differences. American girls of both age groups express most interest in "specialties"—such activi-

Table 3. Occupational Choices of Japanese and American Girls

| | Japanese % | | American % | |
	Grades 1-4	Grades 5-8	Grades 1-4	Grades 5-8
Specialties	6.6	15.3	33.4	39.0
Manual and related	6.6	9.1	3.3	2.0
Teaching	46.4	31.5	21.4	17.3
Arts	20.4	20.0	18.3	12.8
Professions	4.6	4.9	3.1	8.3
Military roles	—	—	0.5	1.1
Sports	1.0	0.3	1.2	1.4
Religious roles	0.5	—	0.8	0.4
Business	7.7	9.4	5.2	11.4
Domestic (house- wife or mother)	4.1	3.9	9.7	3.9
Miscellaneous	2.0	5.7	3.0	2.5
Total	99.9	100.1	99.9	100.1
N	196	406	967	949

ties as nursing, airline hostessing, and to lesser degrees in the roles of the interior decorator, therapist, laboratory technician, librarian, and model. Japanese girls share some of these interests, and they add roles that are ignored by American girls, that is, pharmacist, activities in politics or public office. For Japanese girls the primary interest is in teaching, a field of much less interest to American girls though still an important one for them. Almost one-tenth of the older Japanese girls express interest in the trades (dressmaking, hairdressing, and police work, for example), while very few American girls of either age group do so.

In both countries the girls show considerable interest in the arts and some interest in business and professions. Art interest among American girls usually means dancing, especially ballet. The Japanese girls express a wide variety of artistic interests, both traditional (flower-arranging, drawing, painting, instrumental music) and Western (piano, ballet). Business commands more attention from older girls. In Japan this category means mainly "shopkeeping," while to American girls it means mainly secretarial work. Medicine is the prime professional interest in both countries, but older American girls are concerned also with "science."

Military and religious roles get almost no attention from either Japanese or American girls. Domestic activities are mentioned by about one of ten young American girls, and by much smaller proportions of Japanese and of older American girls.

The child views we have just discussed were elicited predominantly from youngsters of middle-class homes. We also have data gathered from children of lower-class, poverty-area homes in the United States. This latter study, by Beman and Goodman, involved small numbers of urban Mexican-American, Anglo, and Negro children of first through sixth grades.[40] In their replies to an interview question about their own possible future work, we have clues to their awareness of adult work roles.

As might be expected, the range of activities mentioned by these poverty-area children is narrow as compared with the range evident in the responses of middle-class American and Japanese children. We have noted the great variety of occupational roles discussed by the middle-class children, and the great interest shown by the boys in business and the professions. Among the lower-class boys there are few references to the professions and even fewer to business (see Table 4). This is to be expected in view of the restricted social environments of these children. It is difficult to accept as valid the findings from certain studies that seem to show that elementary school children of different social classes show almost no difference in vocational interests. Poverty-area children are unlikely to encounter individuals engaged in a rich variety of high-skill occupational roles, nor do they hear much of the incidental conversation about such roles that is likely to be heard in middle- and upper-class homes.

With the exception of the Negroes, lower-class boys seem aware mainly of "manual and related" occupations. They think especially of the occupational roles of the policeman, and secondarily of the carpenter. The somewhat greater range of occupational awareness suggested by the comments of the Negro boys may well be misleading. It is likely that the Mexican-American and Anglo boys are equally aware of a spectrum of work roles, but that they tend realistically toward a very narrow range when thinking in terms of their own probable futures. In this study, and also in an earlier study made in the same city, we have found among poverty-area Negro children an inclination toward extravagant statements about educational goals.[41] A certain extravagance, an inclination to talk loftily about occupational roles, is in accord. Therefore, we do not regard the findings presented in Table 4 as convincing evidence of greater awareness among Negro boys of adult work activities. These data rather suggest greater realism among Mexican-American and Anglo boys than among Negro boys when the context for discussion of work roles is

**Table 4. Occupational Choices of Mexican-American,
Anglo, and Negro Boys
(Lower Class)**

	Mexican-American	Anglo	Negro	Total
Business	—	1	—	1
Professions	—	1	3	4
Military roles	1		2	3
Manual and related	12	18	4	34
Teaching	—	1	1	2
Religious roles	—	—	—	0
Specialties	—	—	—	0
Sports	—	—	3	3
Arts	—	—	2	2
Miscellaneous or don't know	4	2	1	7
N:	17	23	16	56

their personal future activities. However, the numbers of children studied are too small to provide strong support for these interpretations.

**Table 5. Occupational Choices of Mexican-American,
Anglo, and Negro Girls
(Lower Class)**

	Mexican-American	Anglo	Negro	Total
Business	2	—	2	4
Professions	—	—	1	1
Military roles	—	—	—	0
Manual and related	—	1	1	2
Teaching	—	—	—	0
Specialties	6	12	7	25
Sports	—	—	—	0
Arts	2	2	—	4
Miscellaneous or don't know	7	7	5	19
N:	17	22	16	55

Between the girls of the three groups no comparable disparity appears. However, the Anglo girls incline toward "specialties" (nursing 7, teaching 4, and airline hostessing 1). Almost the same specialties are mentioned by Mexican-American and Negro girls, but the latter stress nursing (nursing 6, teaching 1). "Business" means, in all cases, secretarial work. Roles falling in the "arts" category are ballet dancing (3) and singing (1). The lone "profession" mentioned is "scientist." We have allocated to the "miscellaneous" category mentions of such nonoccupational adult roles as "mother" (9 cases). The girls seem to incline less than the boys toward thought of work roles, and more toward domestic roles, when the discussion is cast in terms of personal future activities. However, we have again rather few children in the study group, and no firm conclusions can be drawn.

Child's-Eye Views of Men: Salient and Preferred Status Attributes

School-age children are likely to be aware of a wide range of social roles and categories and of associated overt signs and symbols. Cultural differences are, of course, reflected in awareness and in preferred categories and attributes. However, "it appears that certain aspects of children's preferences are very widespread," that they are cross-cultural and perhaps universal.[42]

This tentative conclusion is stated by Wayne Dennis, on the basis of his remarkable study of values as expressed in drawings made by children (boys mainly), ages eleven, twelve, and thirteen. Drawings were collected in the United States, Mexico, Great Britain, Sweden, West Germany, Greece, Turkey, Lebanon, Israel, Iran, Cambodia, Japan, and Taiwan. "In several of these countries drawings were obtained from several different ethnic groups, and from both public and private schools, or from both poor and well-to-do neighborhoods."[43] Each of 2,550 boys was asked to draw a man.

The boys show a preference for youthfulness of appearance; that is, few (no more than 5 per cent) in any group drew a wrinkled face, a bald head, or a stooped posture. "The infrequency of drawings of old men, in our opinion, is not the expression of a specific aversion to old age . . . [Rather] it is an instance of a general aversion to men who have defects, whether the defects are due to age, deformity, injury, or sickness . . . Spectacles ordinarily signify the presence of a visual defect."[44] They are shown in the drawings of very few children, and far more frequently in Japan, where they are associated with learning and its associated prestige, than elsewhere. Cross-eyes, eye patches, blindness, facial scars, crippled impairments, obesity, and tattooing are represented only rarely if at all. Perhaps meanness or sadness, suggested by drawing mouths wit¹ the corners turned down, may also be regarded as something oí a defect. In any case, only five of the 2,550 drawings show this feature. Few children made drawings unmistakably intended to show a man in poverty (patched clothing). To be poor is perhaps regarded as a kind of defect too, though a social rather than a physical defect.

It should be noted that several of our groups of boys were poor. Certainly, patches on clothing are not unknown to Mississippi Negro boys or to boys in poor Lebanese villages. Yet not one of these boys drew a man with patched clothing.[45]

Another significant aspect of the drawings is the strong preference shown for "modern dress"—the dress of the Euro-American with shirt, belt, trousers, and shoes. This mode of dress is now known and increasingly preferred almost everywhere in the world, though in places it still competes, or recently competed, with "traditional" costume (for example, with kimono and sandals in Japan). Dennis finds that modern dress is nearly always shown, regardless of the practices still prevailing in the societies to which the young artists belong. This fact tells us a great deal about not only what they prefer now, but about probable future trends. Dennis says:

The wearing of modern dress is part of an encompassing change which may be called "modernization." In our view the boy who draws a modern costume prefers not only modern dress but in all likelihood other, less visible, aspects of modern life . . . . [Probably] further cultural change will occur.[46]

A particularly high incidence of traditional dress was represented by boys in the Sudan and among the Hassidim of Brooklyn. This latter interesting group is made up mainly of "post-World War II imigrants from Hungary who are dedicated to preserving what they consider to be the pious way of Jewish life."[47] But even Hassidic boys are going "modern," in spite of strongly conservative parental and community influences. Some 65 per cent of them drew men lacking the traditional broad-brimmed black hat, the ear curls, and full beard. The majority of Amish boys also drew men in modern dress.

To the children, clothing of the "modern" type is likely to be a symbol of urbanity and of status superior to that of people who wear traditional dress. This status implication is dramatically illustrated in Chiapas, Mexico. Here the urban Ladinos wear modern dress, the rural Indians generally do not. Indeed, upward mobility from Indian to Ladino status can be accomplished in part by altering one's habits with respect to clothing. Dennis collected 400 drawings from Ladino boys. There is among them not a single representation of Indian dress, though it would be easy to draw, and Dennis found the boys quite able to represent Indian dress when he asked them to do so.

Cultural differences are marked with respect to emphasis on masculinity in the drawings. Showing men with mustaches, beards, facial stubble, cigars or pipes, very broad shoulders, canes or weapons, and clothing indicative of masculine occupations—these are the ways in which masculinity is emphasized. Dennis finds that among boys in Heidelberg 71 per cent put one or more of these elements into their drawings; in his other groups the emphasis on these characteristics isn't so high (next highest is a Taipei group, with 59 per cent). Chiapas Indian boys, at the other extreme, represent these features in only 3 per cent of their drawings. Dennis comments:

In view of the high [masculinity] score obtained in Heidelberg we regret that we do not have other German data. We cannot conclude from this set of drawings that there is a masculinity emphasis among Germans in general. However, relevant facts come to mind in respect to the history of the Germanic peoples.[48]

Group differences are even more marked with respect to the incidence of smiling and nonsmiling faces. The "old American" boys (that is, white Christians, several generations in the United States) produced drawings of which 75 per cent had smiling faces. Other Americans, both Christians and Jews, are relatively high in the incidence of smiling faces. Chiapas Indians and Lebanese villagers, by contrast, produced only 5 per cent and 4 per cent, respectively, of smiling faces. The drawings of orthodox Israelis, Athenians, and Mississippi Negroes also show very low incidences. Dennis interprets these intriguing differences as reflective of differing cultural emphases upon happiness as a social goal. Nowhere is this idea so stressed as in the United States, where it is an article of faith that "the American child has a right to enjoyment and almost an obligation to achieve it, and his face should show that happiness is being achieved." Elsewhere in the world "the values of dignity, family pride, seriousness, obedience, respect to elders are still impressed upon the child. Their drawings express this."[49] Dennis concludes, for a variety of reasons, that the facial expressions children draw reflect primarily their "vision of what men should be," rather than their own feelings at the time of the drawing.[50] But the standard of living is also, he suggests, a factor of some importance, though secondary to the culturally patterned expectations.

Another group difference probably traceable to culture is the incidence of diverse social roles in the drawings, that is, of men shown engaged in a variety of activities and occupations. Dennis summarizes the extremes of difference as between the Heidelberg, Edinburgh, and Armenian children, who rather often show variety in social roles, and the Orthodox Israeli, Chiapas Indian, and Lebanese village boys who seldom or never do so (see Table 6).[51]

Table 6. Percentages of Diversified Social Roles in Six Groups

	Heidel- berg	Edin- burgh	Armenians Lebanese	Israeli Orthodox	Chiapas Indians	Lebanese villages
Historical figures	12	1	17	0	0	0
Modern gunmen	19	5	5	1	0	0
Foreigners	6	3	5	0	0	0
Sportsmen, athletes	12	15	7	0	2	0
Entertainers	4	3	1	0	0	0
Occupations	2	10	1	1	0	0
Religious figures	0	1	2	0	0	0
Total	55	38	38	2	2	0

Boys who live in tribal or village cultures are likely to be unaware of a wide range of activities and occupations known to children in urban industrial settings. In the latter contexts the children of the poor are likely to be unaware of many social roles known to children of the middle and upper classes. Yet these facts do not entirely explain the wide discrepancies Dennis reports, nor such anomalies as a low incidence of social role diversity in drawings by "old American" boys.

Work roles are infrequently represented in all the groups. Concerning this rather surprising fact Dennis observes: "one wonders how the world's work gets done, or perhaps we should say that one wonders how it will get done by the next generation."[52] Boys in Edinburgh (a rather poor neighborhood), in Cambodia, and in a Japanese village represent working men in 10, 9, and 8 per cent, respectively, of their drawings. These are the highest incidences. Americans and Germans, who might be expected on cultural grounds to show keen awareness of work and work roles, fail to do so. Dennis advances some possible explanations: boys do not see their fathers at work; many occupations—physicist or mathematician, for example—are not highly visible. But neither suggestion explains the nonrepresentation of work roles that *are* seen (they need not be father's) and which *are* highly visible. The most reasonable explanation would seem to be that if work roles were of absorbing interest they would be represented in drawings.

This theory is supported by the lack of religious emphasis in drawings. Religious content is even less frequent than work content, but that religious content should be low is rather less surprising. Probably boys of eleven to thirteen are in most cultures unlikely to be greatly interested in religious roles, artifacts, or activities. Christians and Jews of several types each, Moslems and Buddhists—all are well represented among the more than 2,500 boys who made drawings; between them all they produced a total of six figures that can be reasonably associated one way or another with religion.

Few of the drawings appear to be intentionally humorous or satirical. A German boy caricatures an American sheriff, a Swedish boy lampoons a pipe-smoking, umbrella-toting Englishman, another Swedish boy draws a ridiculous policeman, a Scottish boy's sketch of a wind-blown old man is delightfully lively, and there are two rather crude caricatures of big-nosed men done by a Beirut boy and an Armenian Lebanese. No other drawings are unequivocally designed to convey ridicule or humor. Drawing skill, or the lack of it, is no doubt a factor limiting productions of this sort, as Dennis suggests. Yet, as he points out, culturally patterned attitudes must be involved. The Japanese boys, for example, draw excellently but wholly without humor.

Relationships Within and Between Age Groups

A powerful and persistent folklore has grown up in the United States concerning children and their relations with "the peer group." This phenomenon might be of merely academic interest were it not that the folklore is widely accepted as fact, even as "scientific" fact, and therefore accepted as a guide for adults in their dealings with children. Here, taken from a highly regarded psychology text on *Childhood and Adolescence*, is a representative statement of the "scientific" folklore:

Parents must adapt to the fact that school-age children are committed to the mores of the peer group. Without the group, the child's growth toward individuality and a sense of self-reliance are endangered. He may over-identify with adult values. . . . It is evident that the peer group is a mixed blessing, but also that it plays an important and perhaps indispensable part in growing up.[53]

90

It is of course important that children have contacts with other children. Among themselves the young share interests and practice skills appropriate to immature and inexperienced members of a society. Because of their similarities in these respects the young tend to communicate easily and to enjoy one another's company. But interest and experience similarities draw together the mature and the elderly as well as the young. That there is a quite natural inclination toward age-grouping is attested by anthropological reports from around the world.

To say these things is not to say that a strong orientation toward the peer group is an "indispensable" part of growing up. Cross-cultural evidence allows no such conclusion, and to argue for it is to demonstrate cultural provincialism. It is indeed to demonstrate an astonishing inclination to equate what is commonplace—but by no means universal—in a given society at a given time with what is inherent and even essential in human nature and to human development. In fact a careful inspection of the here-and-now society would turn up many a child who is not "committed to the mores of the peer group," and whose "individuality and sense of self-reliance" are thereby evident and in process of being strengthened. One need only note such cases as those of nondeliquents grown up in neighborhoods dominated by delinquents, or of exceptionally bright and talented children who grow up as "isolates" (a pejorative label when applied by experts who subscribe to the "indispensable peer group" folklore). Here-and-now societies, the Soviet Union as compared with the United States, for example, are conspicuously different with respect to peer-group influence. There is evidence that Soviet children are "more responsive to the influence of grown-ups than of peers, whereas their American age mates showed a trend in the opposite direction."[54] Moreover, the same study shows that in the Soviet Union peer groups exerted some influence in support of adult standards, whereas in America they encouraged deviance from adult norms.

To caution that the child "may over-identify with adult values" is to express but another facet of contemporary American belief. Among the curious features of our child-centered culture is the notion that nonadult values are somehow inherently better. It is a notion that would astound most of the world's peoples past and even present. Rarely have significant segments of any society questioned whether maturity and experience count for something, whether on average the adult is wiser than the child. This has seemed to most peoples self-evident.

It has been accepted widely too that there are not just "adult values," but values and principles of enduring importance for individuals without regard for age. What a society defines as enduring values it expects adults to hold and to teach. Until they have learned much of what adults have to teach, in the way of knowledge and skills as well as of values, the privileges of adulthood are withheld from the young. These time-tested concepts of childhood and of adulthood are of obvious utility in a viable society.

American experts long have instructed parents and teachers, as do Stone and Church in the statement quoted above. Ours is an expert-oriented as well as a peer-group-oriented society. We listen and, by and large, we believe. So do our children. The young are quick to sense how adults conceive of relationships, what adults do and do not expect of children. American adults expect strong peer-group orientation; they convey this expectation in countless ways. On the whole their expectations are fulfilled. The expert then points to the "proof" of his generalization, which was in fact little more than a self-fulfilling prophecy.

Even within American society, and in face of its manifold pressures toward the peer group, many children do grow up otherwise oriented. We have called attention to the nondelinquent in high delinquency areas and to the individual "loner"—the isolate. There are other examples, children in subsocieties such as the Amish, for instance. Amish children identify not with other children, not with their peers, but with the adult world. Manford Kuhn collected from rural Amish, Mennonite and "Gentile" children, fourth through eighth grades, their views concerning role preferences, rejections, anticipations, and models. He found children of the three groups "remarkably different." And he continues:

. . . the roles preferred by the Amish children were to an astonishing degree roles which we deem to belong to adult world activity. But they also indicated that the roles avoided or rejected by the Amish . . . were also of the adult world. . . . The Amish children named adult objects such as dishes, breeding animals, farmland, and so forth, when asked to name things they now owned which they liked most, . . . while the Gentile children—as we would expect—named toys and playthings.[55]

The key explanation seems to be that the Amish, hence their children as well, do not conceive of a sharply age-graded social universe. Amish children "conceive of themselves as young adults." They in fact play adult roles to a significant degree, and "to a youngster who is playing an adult role, the trinkets of our children must appear as highly superficial placebos."[56]

Kuhn reports a most interesting observation: Amish children command respect from non-Amish children. He writes:

I had been initially interested in studying Amish personality by observing the behavior of three Amish children who had been forced . . . to attend the consolidated school. . . . Despite the peculiarities of their dress and other behavior, they were neither ridiculed nor picked on by the other students. Furthermore, although they did not possess any of the paraphernalia of childhood which we deem appropriate—such as bicycles, ball-playing equipment, multitudinous dolls, mechanical toys, guns, or other gadgets, they seemed utterly serene and happy about their situation. While our children had hours and hours of free time, both before and after school and over the weekends, the Amish children spent this time in chores and farm work and gave little if any evidence of minding, resenting, or rebelling . . . [57]

Kuhn suggests that the "Gentile" children admired the Amish and envied them for their adult roles, "thus the respect and lack of ridicule which our children accord the Amish despite their queer garb."[58]

The Amish identification with adults is reminiscent of other traditional societies in which the kin group almost universally takes precedence over most or even all other groups, peers included. But many preindustrial, pre-urban societies' mistrust of persons outside the kin group is systematically cultivated. In the Mexican village of Las Cuevas, for example:

The chance that [the child] . . . might rebel against [parental] . . . authority and band together with his peers, as children do in the United States and Western Europe, never materializes. Parents discourage play with other children. Futhermore, the society lacks models for fraternal cooperation. Even the games of children . . . lack the symbolic acting-out of the group banding together to home-free-all their comrades from the central authority.[59]

Certain regularities may be noted among these striking contrasts which have been reported here. In many societies, and particularly in those whose cultures are preindustrial and pre-urban, young children assume, to the extent of their physical abilities, the responsibilities of full-fledged citizens. The work skills of adult men and women begin to be practiced as soon as the child can walk. Certain motor developments and coordinations appropriate to the culturally patterned adult roles are emphasized.

The skills and knowledge necessary to meet social obligations and responsibilities are also a part of the culture of early childhood in the traditional societies. Self-control and detailed etiquette with respect to elders, visitors, and neighbors—these patterns are acquired early.

In contrast, an intensive study of urban American four-year-olds (Goodman and Cockrell) shows how different and how relatively few are their obligations and responsibilities. But the large majority does in fact meet culturally patterned expectations with reasonable regularity. A strong orientation toward the self—a preoccupation with I/me/mine as against you/they/theirs—is apparent, reflecting an American cultural emphasis on the private sphere.

We can postulate that the judgments children make are an expression of their general inclination to watch others closely and critically. Concepts about adults—their marital relationships, their work, and other aspects of their lives—are built into the culture of childhood as children watch, listen, and speculate. Vivid illustrations of this process are provided in the life history of an elderly Navaho (Dyk). In modern, urban societies children are likely to have less opportunity to observe details of adult activities, particularly the intimate relations of parents and the work roles of men. Even so, several studies show that children of the middle years have usually quite clear—and quite conventional—concepts of male/female roles generally and of the work performed by their own fathers specifically.

The American culture of childhood, reflecting an American folklore to which child development experts have contributed, puts relatively heavy emphasis on peers. Certain American subsocieties depart from the mode, however. Amish children, for example, identify with adults, not with peers, and indeed conceive themselves as young adults. The pattern is reminiscent of other traditional societies, though in the traditional societies persons outside the kin group may be excluded from the world of trusted adults. Indeed, middle childhood as a clearly demarcated phase of development seems to be uniformly associated only with an urban, industrial type of society.

NOTES

[1] George Bird Grinnell, *The Cheyenne Indians* (New York: Cooper Square Publishers, 1962), I, 115 f.

[2] John G. Neihardt, *Black Elk Speaks* (New York: William Morrow and Co., 1932) p. 92.

[3] *Ibid.*, p. 94.

[4] Oscar Lewis, *Pedro Martinez* (New York, Random House, 1964), p. 15.

[5] *Ibid.*, p. 19.

[6] M. F. Smith, *Baba of Karo, A Woman of the Muslim Hausa* (New York: Philosophical Library, 1955), p. 68.

[7] Marion Pearsall, *Klamath Childhood and Education* (Berkeley and Los Angeles: University of California Press, 1950), p. 348.

[8] Robert Coles, *Children of Crisis* (Boston: Little, Brown and Co., 1964), pp. 326 f.

[9] Otto Raum, *Chaga Childhood* (London: Oxford University Press, 1940), p. 179.

[10] *Ibid.*, p. 158.

[11] *Ibid.*, p. 146.

[12] *Ibid.*, p. 144.

[13] *Ibid.*, p. 145.

[14] Grinnell, *op. cit.*, p. 109.

[15] *Ibid.*, p. 109.

[16] *Ibid.*, p. 108.

[17] Sister M. Inez Hilger, *Chippewa Child Life and Its Cultural Background* (Washington, D.C.: Bureau of American Ethnology, 1951), p. 97.

[18] *Ibid.*, p. 98.

[19] Leo W. Simmons, ed., *Sun Chief—The Autobiography of a Hopi Indian* (New Haven: Yale University Press, 1942), p. 51.

[20] Oscar Lewis, *Tepoztlan—Village in Mexico* (New York: Holt, Rinehart & Winston, 1960), p. 59.

[21] Laurence Wylie, *Village in the Vaucluse* (New York: Harper and Row, 1964) p. 83.

[22] Mary Ellen Goodman and Dura-Louise Cockrell, "Emergent Citizenship—A Study of Four-Year-Olds (mimeographed, 1958).

[23] Walter Dyk, *Son of Old Man Hat* (New York: Harcourt, Brace & Co., 1938), p. 44.

[24] Dorothea Leighton and Clyde Kluckhohn, *Children of the People* (Cambridge, Mass.: Harvard University Press, 1947), p. 88.

[25] Dyk, *op. cit.*, pp. 45 f.

[26] *Ibid.*, p. 48.

[27] Leighton and Kluckhohn, *op. cit.*, p. 54.

[28] Dyk, *op. cit.*, p. 10.

[29] *Ibid.*, p. 17.

[30] *Ibid.*, pp. 17 f.

[31] *Ibid.*, p. 39.

[32] *Ibid.*, p. 34.

[33] *Ibid.*, p. 48.

[34] Hilde T. Himmelweit, A. N. Oppenheim, and Pamela Vince, *Television and the Child* (London: Oxford University Press, 1958), pp. 82 f.

[35] Ruth E. Hartley, "Current Patterns in Sex Roles: Children's Perspectives," *Journal of the National Association of Women Deans and Counselors*, 25 (1961), 3 f.

[36] *Ibid.*, p. 5.

[37] *Ibid.*, p. 8.

[38] Mary Ellen Goodman, "Values, Attitudes, and Social Concepts of Japanese and American Children," *American Anthropologist*, 59 (1957), 979-999.

[39] *Ibid.*, p. 983.

[40] Alma Beman and Mary Ellen Goodman, "Child's-Eye-Views of Life in an Urban Barrio," mimeographed (Houston: Rice University Center for Research in Social Change and Economic Development, 1968).

[41] Mary Ellen Goodman and Douglass Price-Williams, "The People of Census Tract 16," mimeographed (Houston: Rice University, 1965), pp. 27 f.

[42] Wayne Dennis, *Group Values Through Children's Drawings* (New York: John Wiley and Sons, 1966, p. 16.

[43] *Ibid.*, p. 11.

[44] *Ibid.*, p. 18.

[45] *Ibid.*, p. 21.

[46] *Ibid.*, p. 37.

[47] *Ibid.*, p. 38.

[48] *Ibid.*, pp. 93 f.

[49] *Ibid.*, pp. 109 f.

[50] *Ibid.*, p. 112.

[51] *Ibid.*, p. 144.

[52] *Ibid.*, p. 118.

[53] L. Joseph Stone and Joseph Church, *Childhood and Adolescence* (New York: Random House, 1957), p. 224.

[54] Urie Bronfenbrenner, "Response to Pressure from Peers versus Adults among Soviet and American School Children," *International Journal of Psychology*, 2 (1967), 203 f.

[55] Manford H. Kuhn, "Factors in Personality: Socio-Cultural Determinants as Seen Through the Amish," in Francis L. K. Hsu, ed., *Aspects of Culture and Personality* (New York: Abelard-Schuman, 1954), pp. 55 f.

[56] *Ibid.*, p. 59.

[57] *Ibid.*, p. 54.

[58] *Ibid.*, p. 59.

[59] Michael Maccoby, "Love and Authority," *Atlantic Monthly*, 213 (1964), 124.

6

Values and Conscience

Specific habits of obedience give way to
generic self-guidance, that is to say, to
broad schemata of values that confer
direction upon conduct.

Gordon W. Allport

We have noted striking differences between children at opposite poles
of the "citizenship" continuum, between children whose behavioral
patterns are highly negative and others highly positive vis-à-vis the
ideal patterns of their culture. These differences raise again that
ancient and nagging question: Why?

To what extent are such differences a reflection of cultural contexts—a matter especially of values internalized, so that the "self-
guidance" of conscience has developed? To what extent are they psychological—a matter of personality shaped by the interpersonal relations the child has experienced? To what extent are they biocultural
—a matter of the unfolding, in a particular context, of inherent
temperament and inclination?

In this country the study of children and their development long
has been dominated by a radical environmentalism. The possibility
of significant congenital factors has been minimized, if not denied.
This is no longer the case, as the work of Margaret E. Hertzig and
her colleagues (cited earlier) will illustrate. It is clear that a child's
character is the product of more than social and cultural forces.
Inherent capacities and dispositions develop in a field of environmental forces, and in accord with the child's perceptions of these
forces. Dubin and Dubin, reviewing research on children's social
perceptions, comment:

. . . a child's behavior and attitudes do not seem to be closely related to any particular aspect of the home or early environment; they seem, rather, to be determined by the nature of the child and his relation to the total psychological field in which he functions . . . literature on child-training . . . is conspicuous for its lack of attention to the child's "psychological field."[1]

From our point of view the "field" is the total environment— social, cultural, and even physical environment. With that redefinition we fully accept the Dubins' statement.

The inherent and the field factors together, in complex interaction, affect the course of the developing individual, but do not wholly determine it. To this amalgam must be added a final ingredient—the thrust, the autonomy of the individual.

Types of Biocultural Mix and the Cultures of Childhood

In a representative segment of a large society one should expect, on a purely statistical basis, such a distribution of biocultural factors as would result in a bell-shaped curve. What we found in our study of "citizenship" among the middle-class four-year-olds appears to reflect just such a distribution. But in social segments of a less representative sort one should expect a somewhat different distribution. In poverty segments of society, and in segments made up of disadvantaged minorities, one should expect to find abnormally high proportions of children whose "citizenship" patterns diverge significantly from the ideal patterns prevalent in the larger society. This is indeed what teachers, social workers, and researchers often report.

In these "disadvantaged" segments of society, congenital health and nutritional conditions are likely to be inferior. Prevailing cultural patterns—values crucial among them—may be radically divergent from the ideal patterns of the larger society. The biocultural mix therefore is often, but by no means always, conductive to a culture of childhood that is markedly unlike that prevailing in the middle-class, among the children of our nursery school study, for example.

In slums there are two major types of biocultural mix; they are preserved and maintained by two major types of households—the "stable" and the "disorganized." In these contrasting settings two major types of childhood culture are likely to be transmitted—the middle-class type and the impoverished (the culture of poverty) type.

The middle-class type is seldom discussed in reports on the lifeways of children in disadvantaged groups. Oscar Lewis's widely read books describing poverty families of Mexico City, of San Juan, Puerto Rico, and of New York present no hint of a middle-class type.[2] Perhaps there is none. More likely, I think, Lewis elected to study only the impoverished type. He does not tell us which may be the case. But in the slums with which I am familiar the life styles of children and of adults range between middle-class and impoverished. Both polar types are well represented, with difficult-to-classify intermediates represented too. This I have found to be the case without regard for racial or ethnic identities (see Table 7).

**Table 7. Hypothetical Continuum of Household Types
in a "Disadvantaged" Social Segment,
and Associated Cultures of Childhood**

Households	Stable	Intermediates	Disorganized
Cultures of Childhood	Middle-class	Intermediates	Impoverished

Such a continuum has been reported by other observers too.

Pavenstedt (1965) has pointed out that the behavior in nursery school situations of lower-class children from disorganized home environments differs markedly from that observed in children of the same ethnicity and social class who come from stable families and home situations. . . . Because some available data have suggested a high frequency of familial disorganization in lower-class children, a tendency has developed to view these two conditions as synonymous.[3]

Variants of Cultures of Childhood in Disadvantaged Social Segments

There are, however, ethnic variants of the middle-class and of the impoverished cultures of childhood. Beman and Goodman found unmistakable signs of ethnic subcultures cross-cutting both middle-class and impoverished lifeways.[4] Language, dialect, attitudes, and values about paternal authority and intrafamily obligations are a few of the conspicuous elements in which ethnic subcultures differ.

Studies of children in a "disadvantaged" minority—the Maori of New Zealand—also point up this matter of ethnic variants cross-cutting the poverty subcultures. It is reported that among the Maori children, "mother is more significant for the girls and father for the boys, [and] . . . home is, for the boys, an infinitely more desirable place than it is for the girls." The latter "appear to be indifferent to

101

everybody [in the home] except mother whom they like and baby whom they dislike." Boys, on the other hand, tend to "distribute their likes widely through the family . . . [and they] exhibit overt aggressive behavior towards a wide variety of family members."

The father, mother, older sister and younger sister are the objects of this aggression. Sears *et al* . . . also found in the doll play situation that [American] boys showed more aggression towards the father than the mother . . . greater aggression in boys than in girls is the characteristic of children in cultures other than Rakau.[5]

But Arnold Gesell's description of the five-year-old as a "minor tyrant" does not at all fit the Rakau five-year-old. Jane Ritchie says that he is, in fact, "a rather pathetic person, shy, confused, and lacking in confidence."[6]

Maori parents think it important that children be generous, that they share with others. However, the children show little inclination to do so.

There is another report on young Maori children—a report of a radically different sort. It is the work of Sylvia Ashton-Warner, novelist and teacher, who writes of the Maori and *pakeha* (white) children she knew and loved during her years of experience in a New Zealand "infant school" for five- to six- or seven-year-olds. Miss Ashton-Warner is passionate and dedicated; to her eye the Maori children are entracing and their lives tragic. The children as she understands them have not much in common with Mrs. Ritchie's shy and inhibited little people. They are perpetual volcanoes of noise and energy—"talking to each other, playing with each other, fighting with each other and loving each other."

The other trouble with this New Race is their desire to make things. If only they'd sit like the white children with their hands still and wait until they're told to do something and told how to do it.[7]

"Teacher" speaks here appreciatively, not critically. The Maoris, descendants of New Zealand's native peoples, are the victims of race prejudice, and Miss Ashton-Warner sympathizes deeply.

Her evidence concerning children's ideas is offered mainly in the form of their words—the words they selected, by Teacher's invitation—for their early reading and writing lessons. Their own compositions tell something about parents and siblings as the children perceive them, about interpersonal behavior, property rights, and what they regard as good and bad. Irini wrote:

My Father got drunk. And He drank all the beer by He self. And we had a party. . . . Mummy said to Daddy give me that money else I will give you a hiding. Mummy gave me a hiding. . . .

Rongo put this on the blackboard:

Mummy is crying because Daddy hit her in the face. Mummy is going to Nanny's today. Daddy is angry.

On her paper she continues:

. . . . I got wild because Daddy was drunk. Then he hit Rongo.

Rame's family report goes:

I fell out of bed so Daddy
Told Mummy to shiff over.

Matawhero contributes:

Yesterday I came home late. My big brother gave me a hiding. Then I start to cry. Then I have to go to sleep.[8]

It is clear that in their little worlds these children see, and cannot avoid seeing, a great deal of violence, a great deal of drinking, crying, and hitting. Because of Teacher's compassion and her intense rapport with them the children let her know about these aspects of their lives. They are aspects about which the researcher (Ritchie), a relative stranger and no doubt relatively formal and objective, would have been unlikely to hear.

Values and the Transmission of Values in "Advantaged" Families

What children know and feel about values will most likely approximate the ideal patterns of the larger society in that segment which may be called "advantaged." By "advantaged" I do not refer to economic factors primarily, but rather to an optimal biocultural mix.

To test this hypothesis, we studied intensively four "successful families."

This family type is, for our purposes, definable both positively and negatively in terms of cultural consensus. In the positive sense the type is definable in terms of those features attributed to the family [by neighbors, friends, teachers, ministers] which are in accord with the ideal patterns. In the negative sense it is definable in terms of the absence, among features attributed to the family, . . . of antithetical features. . . . Comments about the families [we selected] led us to believe what our observations subsequently supported: that in these families values patterning is strong, clear and coherent, and that the process of values transmission [to children] is well established and has proved effective. In each family there is a preschool child whose enculturation in values we observed in process. Each family has also older children (pre-adolescent and adolescent) whose internalized values were manifest in the day-to-day behavior we observed [in-the-home observation, averaging ten hours per week over four to five months for three families, nine months for a fourth].[9]

In these families the parents exert firm control, but they are also highly nurturant. Both parents spend a great deal of time with their children, and give unmistakable evidence of joy in the relationship. Overt expressions of affection and satisfaction are frequent. The prevailing atmosphere of family life is gay and lively, but not hedonistic.

Notwithstanding our many hours of close observation and many pages of detailed records we found it by no means easy to pinpoint the subtleties of values transmission. We know, however, these things:

1. Transmission occurs both overtly and covertly, explicitly and implicitly.
2. At the covert and implicit levels the processes are diffuse and complex; for example, family "atmosphere" is subtly conducive to the transmission of the values implicit in it.
3. At the overt and explicit levels transmission occurs through parent-child [or child-other authority] interaction *incidents, or chains.*[10]

In these "chains," at the parent and other-authority end, the principal components are (1) information-giving, via definition, instruction, direction, explanation, etc.; (2) incentive-giving, via such positives as praise, encouragement, request, etc., and such negatives as warning, unfavorable judgment, remonstrance, etc.; (3) repetition/reminder, either over time or within a given chain.

At the child's end of the chain, principal components are (1) compliance or noncompliance; (2) ego involvement or action involvement, and (3) echo.

In a given family the chains are highly variable with respect to length and type, but those that occur most frequently are short and information-giving.

Of the chains involving incentive-giving, those of the negative type predominate. However, this is almost the only negative element in the parent-child chains. . . . Repetition/reminder, both over time and within a given chain, are fairly frequent. Explicit praise is infrequent.

The highly predominant component at the child's end of the chain is compliance. Non-compliance is highly infrequent, and in no case terminal to the chain. . . . There are many incidents in which compliance/non-compliance have no relevance, since teaching-learning occurs in many situations other than those involving parent and child in a power and control type of relationship. Therefore the record shows (1) many incidents in which there is no overt response from the child, (2) some in which the child is clearly "going along," that is, he is positively involved (on the ego level or on the action level, perhaps both) with the parents' point of view, and (3) some in which the child explicitly echoes the value(s) expressed by the parent.[11]

The transmission of values in these homes, homes of modern, well-educated, highly urbane people, must depend at base upon ancient and perhaps universally applicable principles. The phenomenon of the interaction chains is surely of universal applicability, and probably their basic types as well. These principles are no doubt relevant in all cultural transmission, whether of values or other aspects of culture.

The contexts in which the child acquires his culture do vary, however, and especially with respect to degree of formality/intentionality and of control exercised by parents and other authority figures. These factors must affect seriously the working of basic principles of cultural transmission. Formal and deliberate instruction increases approximately as cultural complexity increases. Curiously enough, the trend with respect to control appears to be quite the opposite. This trend may be illusory, however. Its appearance in certain complex cultures (China, Japan, and England, for example) is a very recent thing, and it came well after these same societies had developed urban-industrial cultures.

Permissiveness and the Transmission of Values

Permissiveness, as a cultural pattern, is the crucial element with respect to this matter of controls. Permissiveness can and does appear in cultures at all levels of complexity. However, it seems always to be a limited and qualified, or an inadvertent permissiveness, except in our own and a few other complex cultures. The permissiveness of most cultures, both folkish and sophisticated, is limited to the infant and toddler. It amounts to unstinted attention, to providing food and such special favors as sweets and toys in prompt response to the slightest whimper.

105

Among the Klamath Indians, for example, "for the first two or three years of life, the child's every want is supplied. . . ."[12] But in such societies when the next baby comes along, or when custom defines the end of babyhood, a rapid and radical change occurs. The period of permissiveness comes to an abrupt halt. "In about his third year, the [Klamath] child is thrust into active play with his age-mates. He learns that he is expected to be brave, strong, and fearless. . . . If he is lazy or cowardly, he is teased and scolded." Formal instruction, "primarily concerned with demeanor and conduct," is considered a matter of major importance. "Children receive daily lectures on subjects of this nature, and are scolded or whipped when they do not live up to the standards"[13]

Permissiveness is in some societies qualified less by age than by selected aspects of culture. In rural Puerto Rico these contrasts appear:[14]

Permissive Patterns	*Restrictive Patterns*
Late weaning	Abrupt, and sometimes harsh, weaning
Tolerance for eating much or little, and for moving about	Taboo on interrupting adult conversations at table (or elsewhere)
Tolerance for self-selected bedtime	Severe toilet training
Administration of punishments inconsistent	Severe punishment for disobedience; praise and direct rewards rare. Interpersonal aggression "discouraged and usually severely punished
Dependency encouraged (by mothers)	"Clingy" child deplored (by mothers)
Tolerance for nudity of little boys	Anxiety about genital exposure of little girls

Earlier we had occasion to note the courtesy patterns, gestural and linguistic as well, that are a part of the culture of young Javanese children. Yet to an American anthropologist it appears that Javanese treatment of the very young is based on the "idea that permissiveness and gentleness are civilized attributes."[15] However, this treatment reflects also another Javanese idea:

The child before he is five or six is said to be *durung djawa*, which literally means "not yet Javanese." The same phrase is applied to mentally unbalanced persons and to adults who are not properly respectful to their elders. . . . It implies a person who is not yet civilized, not yet able to control emotions in an adult manner. . . .[16]

The permissiveness shown the little Javanese person is limited, and it is also qualified by this concept of developmental stages in childhood. Before five or six the capacity fully to accept "civilization" simply is not in the child; therefore only limited demands are made by Javanese adults. The attitude is highly protective:

Since frustration and disappointment are thought to bring about the state of startle *(kaget)*, there is a constant maternal endeavor either to give the child what he wants or to manipulate the situation by distracting his attention or concealing things so that he will not ask for them.[17]

In Japan I have observed "maternal endeavor" of just these sorts. Japanese patterns of limited and qualified permissiveness, and of concepts with respect to age-linked capacities, appear to be quite similar.

In the middle class urban American society there are "three models of parental control—permissive, authoritarian, and authoritative . . ." The first of these models, based largely on psychoanalytic assumptions, has enjoyed a great vogue. "The ideal home or school in the late forties and fifties was organized around unlimited acceptance of the child's current needs for gratification, rather than around adult life. The child was to be granted maximum freedom of choice and self-expression in both settings."[18] This point of view rests on the truly fantastic assumption that control by adults is necessarily to the child's disadvantage. It fails to differentiate between harsh and rigid—that is, authoritarian—control, and that judicious, loving, and firm control which is meant by the term "authoritative."

After a thorough review and summary of the quite extensive relevant research literature, Baumrind concludes that "authoritative [*not* authoritarian] control can achieve responsible conformity with group standards without loss of individual autonomy or self-assertiveness."[19] However, the defenders of the permissive model make contrary assumptions. In fact, the debate easily could have been settled by reference to the anthropological literature; parents around the globe and through the centuries have documented more than adequately this conclusion so belatedly supported by the labors of a small army of psychologists.

Values and Conscience

With the internalization of controls, and their associated values and standards, there develops that moral-ethical gyroscope we call conscience. Defenders of the permissive model exhibit great anxiety lest conscience become too strong, a result certainly not likely as an outcome of permissive rearing. Contemporary urban society in this country, and in some others as well, provides us with massive evidence that prevalent types of problem children suffer from quite the opposite problem—from gross underdevelopment of the conscience. "A child with a weak conscience is one who continues to require external controls—by policemen—and who develops little that can be recognized as adult values or ideals. In adulthood, he contributes himself to the shiftless, irresponsible, criminal part of the population."[20]

Probable failures and inadequacies in conscience and character development often can be predicted in the preschool years. "High predictive accuracy (c. 90 per cent) had been verified in tests conducted in France, Japan, and the United States. The predictive scale used in these tests was developed in the United States by Sheldon and Eleanor Glueck. . . ."[21] The Gluecks, who are famed Harvard Law School criminologists, "occupy a unique place in the history of prediction. They have for some thirty odd years been engaged in prediction research. Their Social Prediction Table was designed to distinguish potentially delinquent boys from pseudodelinquents and nondelinquents as early as the age of six."[22] It has been demonstrated that highly reliable predictions can be made on the basis of three factors: supervision of boy by mother, discipline of boy by mother, and cohesiveness of family.[23]

By age ten character development is far advanced and has assumed its enduring proportions. This fact has been substantiated by Robert Peck and Robert Havighurst[24] who identify these basic character types:

1. *Amoral*: the clinically "psychopathic personality; may be delinquent or merely 'charming but irresponsible'. . . . He has no conscience or superego."[25]

2. *Expedient*: self-centered. Concerned only with "getting." "He behaves in ways his society defines as moral, only so long as it suits his purpose. . . . He has no internalized moral principles, no conscience or superego."[26]

3. *Conforming*: major internalized principle: "to do what others do, and what they say one 'should' do. . . . A Conformist may fre-

quently ignore chances for personal advantage, if they require departure from the prescribed rules of conduct."[27]

4. *Irrational-Conscientious*: "judges a given act according to his own internal standard of right and wrong." More concerned with his definitions than with effects on others. "This is the 'blind,' rigid superego at work."[28]

5. *Rational-Altruistic*: "has a stable set of moral principles by which he judges and directs his own action; he objectively assesses the results of an act in a given situation, and approves it on the grounds of whether or not it serves others as well as himself. . . . He has a strong, firm conscience or superego, but he tests, modifies, and applies its directives in order to achieve the ultimate purpose of the rules it contains."[29]

Peck and Havighurst find these character types, in states of partial development, at any rate, among the urban American adolescents whose families and personal histories they studied closely. However, their theoretical formulations reflect strongly what I have identified as fallacious assumptions—the fallacy of universal age/stage linkages, and the underestimation fallacy. They regard their five character types as developmental phases succeeding one another in the order in which the types are listed. It is assumed that preschool children are not capable of the "highest" of these types (Rational-Altruistic), and that even the Conforming type is associated with "middle and late childhood."[30] Adolescents and adults whose character types fall below the Rational-Altruistic therefore have simply bogged down (become fixated) in one of these earlier developmental phases.

The theory is untenable in light of much evidence (the Goodman-Cockrell "citizenship" study, for example). It does not square with a vast body of anthropological reporting, nor with commonplace observation and experience. Margaret Mead speaks for the anthropologists when she says that cross-cultural variation is so great as to "make any idea of general stages appear useless."[31] It is true that four-year-olds—American, Japanese, Hopi, or whatever—whose "citizenship" patterns are predominantly of the "positive" (Goodman) or of the "Rational-Altruistic" (Peck and Havighurst) types lack such full and mature development of the type as may appear in adults. But the young child/adult discrepancy is surely a matter not of kind, but of degree. To state, or even to imply, that children of preschool age are capable of no more than amorality or expediency is to perform a quite remarkable trick. It involves either mutilating the facts to make them fit the Procrustean bed of theory or performing some sleight-of-hand that causes inconvenient facts to disappear. The result, in either case, is distortion of a sort by no means peculiar to Peck and Havighurst. Numerous others (Lawrence Kohlberg, for example)[32] following in the footsteps of Freud and, more particularly, of J. M. Baldwin and of J. Piaget, have accepted uncritically the age/stage assumptions set forth long ago by these authorities. But we now are seeing a significant decline in adherence to propositions resting heavily on the truth-by-assertion method of verification, or on data drawn only from the United States or another Western society.

NOTES

[1] Robert Dubin and Elizabeth Ruth Dubin, "Children's Social Perceptions: A Review of Research," *Child Development* 36 (1965), 812.

[2] *Five Families* (New York: Basic Books, 1959); *The Children of Sanchez* (New York: Random House, 1961); *La Vida* (New York: Random House, 1965).

[3] Margaret E. Hertzig et al., "Class and Ethnic Differences in the Responsiveness of Preschool Children to Cognitive Demands," *Monographs of the Society for Research in Child Development,* 33 (1968), 3.

[4] Alma Beman and Mary Ellen Goodman, "Child's-Eye-Views of Life in an Urban Barrio," mimeographed (Houston: Rice University Center for Research in Social Change and Economic Development, 1968).

[5] Jane Ritchie, *Childhood in Rakau* (Wellington, N. Z.: Victoria University College Publications, 1957), pp. 118 f.

[6] *Ibid.,* p. 129.

[7] Sylvia Ashton-Warner, *Teacher* (New York: Simon & Schuster, 1963), p. 104.

[8] *Ibid.,* pp. 179-182.

[9] Mary Ellen Goodman and Judy Meyer, "Values and the Transmission of Values in 'Successful Families,' " (mimeographed, 1963), pp. 10-13.

[10] *Ibid.,* p. 145.

[11] *Ibid.,* p. 147.

[12] Marion Pearsall, "Klamath Childhood and Education," *Anthropological Records,* 9 (1950), 350.

[13] *Ibid.,* p. 350.

[14] David Landy, *Tropical Childhood* (Chapel Hill: University of North Carolina Press, 1959), pp. 233-236.

[15] Hildred Geertz, *The Javanese Family* (New York: The Free Press of Glencoe, 1961), p. 95.

[16] *Ibid.,* 105.

[17] *Ibid.,* 106.

[18] Diana Baumrind, "Effects of Authoritative Parental Control on Child Behavior," *Child Development,* 37 (1966), 888.

[19] *Ibid.,* p. 905.

[20] Robert R. Sears, "The Growth of Conscience," in Ira Iscoe and Harold Stevenson, eds., *Personality Development in Children* (Austin: University of Texas Press, 1960), p. 98.

[21] Mary Ellen Goodman, *The Individual and Culture* (Homewood, Ill.: The Dorsey Press, 1967), p. 234.

[22] Maude M. Craig and Selma J. Glick, "Ten Years' Experience with the Glueck Social Prediction Table," *Crime and Delinquency,* July, 1963, pp. 249-250.

[23] *Ibid.*, pp. 258-260.

[24] Robert F. Peck and Robert J. Havighurst, *The Psychology of Character Development* (New York: John Wiley and Sons, 1960).

[25] *Ibid.*, p. 5.

[26] *Ibid.*, pp. 5 f.

[27] *Ibid.*, pp. 6 f.

[28] *Ibid.*, p. 7.

[29] *Ibid.*, p. 8.

[30] *Ibid.*, p. 7.

[31] Margaret Mead in J. M. Tanner and Barbel Inhelder, eds., *Discussions on Child Development* (New York: International Universities Press, 1960), p. 49.

[32] Lawrence Kohlberg, "The Development of Children's Orientations Toward a Moral Order, Part I," *Vita Humana*, 6 (1963), 11-33.

7

Concepts and Knowledge

Most basically, a culture is a conception of
reality and how it works.

Joseph Church

We turn now to those aspects of the culture of childhood in which
the content and processes are primarily of a cognitive order. No hard
and fast line can be drawn, but our focus here is in contrast with
the heavily attitudinal and affective patternings (self and others,
responsibilities, values) we have discussed in the three preceding
chapters.

The Culture of Science vs.
the Culture of Childhood

The view that there is a substantial realm of cognitive patterning, even for very young children, remains still academically unconventional. For the conventional age/stage theorists it is a logical im-
possibility; their theories arbitrarily rule out cognitive richness in
early childhood.

Developmental and psychodynamic theory especially defines the nature of
the young child as rather fragile, autistic, and irrational—at the mercy of
his emotional life. It is also believed that he lacks perceptual-cognitive
structure, objectivity, and basic concepts essential for assimilating cognitive stimuli to any important degree.[1]

We have here neither space nor inclination for a speculative
essay on determinants of the culture of science. But it must prove
instructive should someone examine the forces that have worked to
bring into existence, and even into wide acceptance, theories so re-

113

moved from readily observable child behavior. It must be, as Harlow says, that "many psychologists have children, and these children always behave in accord with the theoretical position of their parents." Those theoretical positions include not only the anticognitive, but that related extremism—behaviorist theory. The behaviorist attributes nothing to the individual and his inherent capacities and interests, everything to environment, biological drives, and conditioning. Harlow, having for eleven months observed his own baby, comments:

Perhaps the most striking characteristic of this particular primate has been the power and the persistence of her curiosity-investigatory motives. . . . The frustrations of Mary X appeared to be in large part the results of physical inability to achieve curiosity-investigatory goals. . . . Can anyone seriously believe that the insatiable curiosity-investigatory motivation of the child is a second-order or derived drive conditioned upon hunger or sex or any other internal drive? The S-R [stimulus-response] theorist and the Freudian psychoanalyst imply that such behaviors are based on primary drives. An informal survey of neobehaviorists who are also fathers (or mothers) reveals that all have observed the intensity or omnipresence of the curiosity-investigatory motive in their own children. None of them seriously believes that the behavior derives from a second-order drive.[2]

Harlow does not tell us whether these same "neobehaviorists" who recognize cognitive activity in their own children then proceed to appropriate alteration of their theories. Certainly many theorists hold long and tenaciously to the conventional position. Apparently, they fail to perceive evidence of early cognitive capacities, inclinations, and achievements. The failure may be due in part to the practice of substituting the laboratory and contrived situations for "real life" observations and the study of children in natural situations.

The substitution is conducive to errors. Barbara Biber and her research colleagues, reporting on their intensive school study of seven-year-olds, comment on the "quality and relative maturity of their conceptual thinking." This evaluation rests on records of spontaneous lunch-time conversations. Biber and her fellow researchers admit that these data have their shortcomings; they do not provide a basis for "an anatomy of ideas or concepts, in general," and their progressive development. Problem-solving and question-answer method may be necessary, but these researchers have misgivings about the fruits of such methods. They write:

All too often, the methods involving direct questioning of children, illus-

114

trated by the work of Piaget, involve a spurious factor which renders certain conclusions ambiguous. . . . A given child's reply, attributed to an intellectual confusion or even to some immature a-logical thought structure, may be a product of feelings of anxiety or compulsion which propel the child toward making *some* answer. . . . Spontaneous conversations do not involve this spurious factor but are restricted as to what they will yield.[3]

Although countertrends have prevailed among scholars, there have been in the last forty years sporadic signs of awareness that children have minds and use them. Susan Isaacs' fine study, *Intellectual Growth in Young Children,* was first published in 1930, and in 1966 it was republished in paperback.[4] Significant studies are now being made by William Fowler[5] and a good many others.[6] It is fortunately true that "we seem to be rediscovering in our research and theory the mind of the child. . . ."[7]

Evidences of Early Cognitive Capacities and Inclinations

In all societies young children command a repertoire of concepts and of knowledge. The content of these repertoires inevitably varies widely, in accord with the distribution of many differences among cultures. But concepts and knowledge are aspects of all cultures. They are aspects of each culture of childhood as well as of its larger counterpart borne by the adults of that society. Children, like their elders, must meet and deal with their world in conceptual terms; "concepts serve as crucial links between the environment and the individual. They are intellectual tools that man uses in organizing his environment and attacking his problems."

When man employs concepts, he thinks in terms of symbols and classes. When he orders diversity into classes or categories, he begins to reduce ambiguity and imprecision.[8]

In his review of research concerning the "attainment of concepts" by children, Sigel discusses especially these types: "concepts organizing apparent relationships of the physical world—object permanence, space, form, color and size [and] those depicting relationships of physical and natural phenomena—causality, mass, weight, and volume." We are concerned with a broader range of phenomena—with concepts of the social realm as well as the physical. We are concerned also with a broader—a cross-cultural—range of data. Sigel, like many psychologists, reports on "the child" without regard for the society or subsociety to which he may belong. In

115

fact, of course, "the child" subjects of most conceptual studies have been American urban middle-class or Western European (especially the Swiss urban middle-class subjects of Jean Piaget's much discussed studies). These are perfectly acceptable subjects; however, as Piaget himself now recognizes, one is not justified in identifying their conceptual behavior as necessarily representative of all children, everywhere.[9] Certain aspects of their behavior are undoubtedly universal; certain others are peculiar to their time and place, their society and subsociety. And the behavior of each child will be also, in certain specifics, unique and peculiar to that individual alone.

Our interest centers upon the universal and the cultural levels. Lacking abundant cross-cultural studies, one's statements about "the child"—about the universals of childhood conceptual behavior—must be limited and qualified. The resulting statements will lack that ring of certainty which is to the unwary the hallmark of ultimate truth. But qualified statements are, in fact, much better approximations of truth than what is sometimes offered us. The cross-cultural data needed as a basis for valid generalizations are admittedly too few. However, even a sampling of these resources will serve to illustrate again the conceptual richness and variety of which very young children are capable.

We have noted (earlier in this chapter and in Chapter 1) evidence of curiosity—investigatory behavior from early infancy, and the selective attention given by the very young to patterns and novelties. There is evidence too that children ask more questions when confronted with things or situations they find novel, surprising, incongruous, or uncertain.[10] Questioning is itself evidence of intellectual seeking (except, of course, that variety of questioning which is used by a child merely to focus attention on himself.) "Questioning is a form of *epistemic behavior*, that is, behavior directed toward, and reinforced by, acquisition of knowledge."[11] The study shows, as one might expect, that older children (Grade 5, urban middle-class Canadian), as compared with kindergarten and primary graders, ask more questions and their questions are more precisely formulated to satisfy their needs for information. Overt thoughtfulness—reasoning about perplexing questions—appears in very young children but is predictably more complex in older ones. Isaacs reports instances in English urban children from three and a half. She comments:

The difference between the younger child and the older, between the child and the adult, is . . . *not* that the former do not reason, or reason *only* in the form of the perceptual judgment and practical manipulation. It is rather

116

the extent to which, with the younger children, the higher forms of noetic synthesis rest directly upon and grow immediately out of the simpler. Verbal reasoning and the clear formulation of judgments are no more than wave-crests upon the flow of young children's thought. They spring up from a practical or personal situation, and die down again to it.[12]

Do children in "primitive" societies reason and ask questions and in these ways seek knowledge? They do. An early (1906) report on African Kafir infants and children mentions these examples of sophisticated questions: "Is this body my real me?" "Have we changed from the people we were yesterday?" "What is it in me that does the thinking?"[13] Questions of these sorts are said to be unusual coming from the Kafir children, but it is important to note that they are asked even rarely in this society. The culture is not conducive to speculation, and children inclined toward it are discouraged by their elders. Inherent curiosity is surely as natural to children in tribal as in modern urban societies. But in either case the cultural climate, and each child's particular exposures to it, can be expected to influence his questioning and his reasoning. Where questions are answered, where children are approved or praised for seeking information, its pursuit is likely to be sustained and vigorous. If one knows what child behaviors are being rewarded in a society, one can infer both the values of the adults and the future behavior of the children.[14] Behavior considered praiseworthy varies greatly between societies, and within them between ethnic and social class segments.

A high frequency of verbal give-and-take, along with other stimuli (such as an ample supply of books in the child's world), are on the whole conducive to sustained curiosity and information-seeking.[15] In a modern urban setting these and other favoring conditions are more likely to be met in the middle class than in the lower class. A recent study of six- and seven-year-old children of both classes, both sexes, and of four ethnic groups (Chinese, Jewish, Negro, and Puerto Rican) lends support to this view. It was found that "middle-class children are significantly superior to lower-class children on all scales and subtests." These measures were selected to identify competence and patterns with respect to verbal ability, reasoning, number facility, and space conceptualization.[16]

The middle-class English children observed by Susan Isaacs in her school showed impressive competence in such cognitive functions. She reports that children not yet five demonstrated "strong and spontaneous . . . [interest] in the things and events of the physical world" around them. Isaacs adds:

We did not "teach" our children about these things, nor try to create an inter-

117

est in them. . . . It was the behaviour of the children themselves, and their
eager questions about cooking, about water and snow and ice and the garden
bonfire, about the drains and the gas pipes and hot-water pipes and electric
light, that led me gradually to give them material that would allow of these
interests being followed out. . . .[17]

Remarkably sophisticated reasoning, and clear verbal formulations of it, were evident along with these and other interests. A boy
not yet six offered succinct explanations about the steepness of
stairs and the working of a bicycle. Other children of the same age
understood a wide range of basic physical principles (for example,
the relationship between pressure and the rise of water) and were
able spontaneously to generalize the principles from one concrete
situation to another.[18] Isaacs comments that according to Piaget
these children were much too young to have any understanding of
mechanical causality.

Reasoning was evident also in comments on social causalities
and relationships. Often these comments fastened, debater style,
on a point of logic the child was exploiting for his own purposes.
The pattern is familiar to all parents and teachers: for example, the
adult proposes sweetly that "we must pick up and put away our playthings so they won't get stepped on and broken." The child (as in
Isaacs' group) points out triumphantly: "We shouldn't break those
big bricks, should we?"[19] Or, like Isaacs' Ursula, the child mercilessly
lampoons an adult's slip from logic:

"Mary's mummie said such a silly thing when I was at school. . . . One day,
when you didn't come early to fetch me, and I didn't want to put on my
things, she said, 'Isn't your mummie late?' And she said, 'If you put on your
things, she'll come quicker.' That couldn't make any difference. . . . Wasn't
that silly? . . ."[20]

Culture and Sensory Categories,
Perceptions, and Selective Attention

Data such as these from Isaacs are unfortunately rare in anthropological reports. But detailed accounts of the behavior of tribal children allow us to make with some confidence inferences concerning their modes of reasoning, their patterns of perception and
conceptualization. Margaret Mead, commenting upon both the difficulties and the fascinations inherent in studies of the thought of
"primitive children," pointed out long ago certain significant cultural
variables.

118

The first group of problems under this head might be concerned with categories, linguistic categories and the ways in which sense experience is classified by non-Indo-European cultures. The need of some such check becomes apparent when we scrutinize studies of musical discrimination, color perception, or such investigations as Piaget made into children's methods of reasoning....

Manus children under five or six were able to repeat a simple melody, but above that age . . . they heard nothing but varying time and stress in a melody, repeating it in a monotone, quite deaf to differences in pitch. Similarly, their color classifications are so different that they saw yellow, olive-green, blue-green, gray, and lavender as variations of one color....

Studies of the dreams of primitive children should yield data on the types of imagery and the degree to which cultural patterns shape the dreams of young children. In Manus, children of six sometimes dream messages from the spirits—a strictly cultural pattern.[21]

Mead noted too that child curiosity, its intensity and the directions it most commonly takes, are affected by culture. She tells us that Manus children do not ask "why." Their attention is focused rather on the "how," "when," and "where" questions. This she sees as understandable in view of the general cultural emphasis "upon physical skill and the manipulation of material things, combined with a lack of interest in origins. . . ."[22]

In cultures lacking either philosophical or scientific focus on origins and causalities the cultural emphases tend to parallel those of Manus. Social skills are often emphasized more than in Manus, but in tribal settings generally the cultures of childhood are weighted on the side of the practical. Survival knowledge and skills such as hunting, gardening, animal husbandry, combat, care of children and the sick, are necessarily emphasized strongly. But in many tribal societies young children pay equal attention to culturally valued social skills.

A perennial amusement among Ngoni boys [Malawi] of five to seven was playing at law courts. They sat round in traditional style with a "chief" and his elders facing the court, the plaintiffs and defendants presenting their case, and the counsellors conducting proceedings and cross-examining witnesses. In their high squeaky voices the little boys imitated their fathers whom they had seen in the courts, and they gave judgments, imposing heavy penalties and keeping order in the court with ferocious severity.[23]

With equal concentration, Ngoni children "from three and four years upwards" watched and practiced a highly demanding form of dancing.

On the edge of the main group small boys particularly would practice steps

119

and postures with intense solemnity and exaggerated movements, singing meanwhile. The Ngoni used no drums and no musical instruments in their dancing, and despised the users of drums. All their rhythm and synchrony was achieved by perfect unison of action and voice. The little boys practicing solo on the edge of a dance group listened intently every now and then to get the rhythm correctly, shifted their feet, and stamped with the rest.[24]

To be a polished and persuasive talker, even an orator, is a social skill prized and pursued by the children in many tribal societies. The Araucanians of Chile strive to perfect the *koyaqtun*—a long, formal discourse made up largely of stylized compliments and questions. Describing Araucanian child life Hilger says:

Oratory is highly esteemed; so is the facility to speak well on all occasions and the ability to carry on a koyaqtun. Formerly every boy was trained in all three; many are still so trained . . . "If a boy was bashful or unable to talk well to people, he was taken into the woods and made to stand on the stump of a roble chileno [because it has the biggest stump] and told to talk from there to trees and plants and animals as though they were human beings . . . "

The sons of a cacique were given special training, not only in oratory but in memorizing, also. The cacique who excelled all other caciques in eloquence and memory and speech-making abilities was respected throughout the Araucanian country as its most renowned and intelligent leader—no higher compliment could be paid him.[25]

Culture and Boy-Girl Differences
in Interests and Knowledge

Curiously enough, the sex differences evident in these examples are by no means unusual. Little girls have always their distinctive patterns in the culture of childhood, but these patterns seldom include the more sophisticated knowledge and skills, the more refined conceptualizations. This statement by Shimkin, about the Shoshone Indians of Wyoming, appears to be true throughout the tribal world, and beyond it as well: "most men [have] enjoyed far greater intellectual activity and possessed far broader mental horizons than most women."[26]

Note, for example, this illustration. It comes from a brief autobiography provided by a Walapai Indian. The informant recalls: "when I was old enough to talk my father made me rise before the sun and go hunting with him or track our horses and bring them into camp." He goes on to tell in some detail the specifics he learned, specifics of hunting each of a variety of animals. And there was much more, including star lore, which his father painstakingly taught this

120

boy. "My father told me, 'I want you to notice the stars, for this reason. Notice this constellation, this marks the beginning of winter. . . .'" Other seasons similarly were identified. Moreover, the father took the child on long rides "to teach me different things and places." No effort was spared to educate and inspire this boy child. And what, if anything, did the same father do to educate and inspire his daughters? He said to them: "'Get up early; get water; cook and be a good housewife.'"[27]

Such radical divergence between the sexes, however one may wish to explain it, is a reality in most cultures, both the relatively simple and the complex. The current American sociocultural system provides to a most unusual degree for equality of the sexes. Even under the favoring circumstances, however, the outlook and interests of girls and boys diverge markedly, and the divergence only widens with age. Individual exceptions notwithstanding, Shimkin's statement seems to hold for the large majorities of men and women in most cultures, if not in all.

Culture and World View

In all cultures the concept and knowledge systems of both boys and girls include a world view—a set of assumptions and beliefs falling in the domains of philosophy or religion. Anthropologists find evidence that these patterns, though they have to do largely with the abstract and intangible, appear in at least rudimentary form in the cultures of early childhood.

Reporting on their intensive study of Navaho children, C. Kluckhohn and D. Leighton comment: "Probably by the time the Navaho child is six months old typically Navaho conceptions of life have begun to permeate and to attain a sway which will last forever." These children learn very early that life is precarious and hard. In their first few years many become personally acquainted with hunger, with severe illness, and with death as it strikes in the kin group.[28] They see how their elders attempt to cope with these hazards, and that their final defenses are "prayers, songs, and ceremonials." And they discover man-made hazards—"whispers about witchcraft"—fear of certain tribesmen.

The child naturally comes to feel that the important thing in life is to be safe. In terms of the supernatural world, this means being careful to do certain things and being equally careful not to do others. In terms of the human world it means carefully following out his share of the expected reciprocities with his relatives.[29]

121

Though inhabited by mysterious, unseen powers the insubstantial world can be very real and taken quite for granted by a young child. Little Winnebago Indian children would stand under the trees "and look at the stars and cry to the Thunders." Mountain Wolf Woman remembers:

When father returned from hunting in the evening he used to say to us, "Go cry to the Thunders." . . . This is what we used to sing:
"Oh, Good Spirits
Will they pity me?
Here I am, pleading." . . .

We used to think we were pitied.[30]

The concept of the Thunder Spirits, and the ritual appropriate for an appeal to them, were distinctive parts of the Winnebago tradition. Winnebago children have also shared an experience very common to children in many cultures through time and space. Wolf Woman recalls:

. . . when we had finished eating [the evening meal] we put the dishes away. Then father used to say, "All right, prepare your bedding and go to bed and I will tell you some stories." . . . He used to tell myths, the sacred stories. . . . Everybody, the entire household, was very quiet and in this atmosphere my father used to tell stories.[31]

Extraordinarily subtle concepts can be sensed by young children. Philosopher Rufus M. Jones recalled the rural Quaker meetings that were a part of his early childhood, and what that rarified atmosphere conveyed to him. He wrote:

There was no bell, no organ, no choir, no pulpit, no order of service, no ritual. There was always silence and then more silence. . . . This "silence of all flesh" was a sacrament of awe and wonder. They [adults] were in faith and practice meeting with God. . . . The silence came over us [children] as a kind of spell . . . a sense of divine presence, which even a boy could feel. It was almost never explained to us. There was very little said about it.[32]

The young child who senses such insubstantialities as a "divine presence" or a "good spirit" is not likely to be inventing; he is likely to be reproducing the concepts of his culture. Children may create fantasy playmates and sometimes think of their dolls as "real." But they are not necessarily more animistic—more inclined to endow trees or rocks or other natural phenomena with indwelling spirits—than are adults.

122

Psychologists unfamiliar with childhood in non-Western cultures have assumed animism to be a childlike mode of conceptualization. In *Growing Up in New Guinea* Margaret Mead has argued, however, that "personalizing the universe is not inherent in child thought, but is a tendency bequeathed to him by his society. . . ."

Children are not naturally religious, given over to charms, fetishes, spells, and ritual. They are not natural story tellers, nor do they naturally build up imaginative edifices. They do not naturally consider the sun as a person nor draw him with a face. [Footnote: In thirty thousand drawings, not one case of personalizing natural phenomena or inanimate objects occurred.] Their mental development in these respects is determined not by some internal necessity, but by the form of the culture in which they are brought up.[33]

Mead reports that the adults of Manus society do not believe that children are imaginative or that they might like to hear stories, and the children fulfill the adult expectations. The nature of Manus language is an important factor too: "All the impetus to personalization which our rich allusive language [English] suggests to a child (the moon smiles, hides, peeps, for example) is absent."[34]

Mead is by no means alone in these views; "the findings of Havighurst and his group . . . with relation to American Indians [show] that a characteristic animism does not decrease with the age of the child but, rather, increases." In fact, says Singer:

It [animism] really is not an infantile mode of perception at all but is culturally determined. I am not saying this is definitive, but I think there are other studies of Western children that have shown that certain of the characteristics which Piaget thinks are developmentally early do not decrease with age but may actually increase.[35]

Of culturally patterned concepts concerning the supernatural, none is more pervasive among American Indians than the guardian spirit concept.

In order to survive in a dangerous world, a growing child in the old [Chippewa] culture had to search for supernatural allies. Soon after he was able to walk and play by himself, a little boy was sent out into the woods to secure a guardian spirit. Until he finally did obtain a fasting dream of vision [in which his personal guardian spirit was identified] he was periodically sent off to fast and wait for a tutelary spirit.[36]

Culture and Conceptualization

We are all aware, if only because of what we have heard, that people who are not "our" kind are different. It is not only that they behave differently; they think differently, as well. Few of us have failed to accept also the corollary implication—"their" behavior and thinking are inferior to "ours."

In fact we may be quite as right about the existence of differences as we are hasty and fallible in attempting to judge whose ways are superior. The latter judgment is not for the hasty nor for the amateur. But the existence of great cultural differences in both behavior and thinking is of course an unarguable fact. Behavior differences are relatively easy to see and to describe. Differences in styles of thinking—in patterns of conceptualization—are much less easy to identify, however sure we may be that they do indeed exist.

Two distinguished anthropologists, Alfred Kroeber[37] and S. F. Nadel,[38] long ago commented upon this phenomenon, and Nadel studied it. Taking leads from Nadel's work I searched for conceptualizing habits in samples of 681 American and 239 Japanese urban middle-class children. All were in the fifth or sixth grades.

This study is a large-scale replication of Nadel's investigation focused on groups of youth in the West African Yoruba and Nupe societies (twenty subjects, twelve to eighteen years of age, in each). Nadel tested the hypothesis that a people will develop thoughtways which reflect and accord with the implicit premises, emphases, and values patterned in their culture.[39]

I utilized, with minor modifications, Nadel's method—the story-recall. Conceptualizing habits are deduced from the forms in which the children reproduce, after a time lapse, a short dramatic story.

The Nupe and Yoruba studies by Nadel showed modal thought-ways (conceptualizing habits) of sorts consistent with the respective cultures. Yoruba culture is relatively systematizing (Kroeber's term), i.e., generalizing, recognizing, and dealing in relations. Yoruba subjects showed more inclination than Nupe to reproduce story material in an organized and rational fashion. Nupe reproductions showed more specificity. Kroeber suggests that these types, which are identified as "rational" and "sensory" respectively, are recognizable also among American Indian peoples.

Data from the present study indicate that Americans are somewhat more systematizing than Japanese. This finding is in accord with what was anticipated in view of the nature of the two cultures, for example, the systematizing influence stemming from

124

American cultural emphasis on ideologies both religious and scientific—emphases not paralleled in Japan. However, there are unanticipated findings as well.

It is surprising, for example, that Yoruba appear to be more systematizing in their conceptual habits than either Americans or Japanese. Kroeber supposes all "advanced" cultures to be of the systematizing type relative to less advanced cultures. We seem to have, in the Yoruba, an exception to the generalization. Whether this is true, and whether this case is unique, can only be determined by further studies and by more refined comparative analysis of data drawn from Yoruba, Japanese, American, and ultimately other societies.

Among unanticipated findings we note also that the Japanese, as compared with the Americans, are somewhat less accurate in reproducing story items, particularly with respect to the body of the story. However, when interpreted in the light of other findings, this fact supports an inclination that was anticipated for Japanese, that is, the inclination toward recall of a nonsystematized type, through attempted rote memorization of specifics. The supporting findings are: high Japanese accuracy at the beginning and end of the story; stronger inclination of Japanese to reproduce verbatim or nearly so; less inclination to add, modify, or paraphrase; less inclination to depart from the original sequence of events.

Certain other trends in Japanese reproductions are less easily interpreted; for example, the Japanese are no more given than Americans to recall the fact of the younger brother's refusal to give up the girl loved by his elder brother too, or the ensuing violent quarrel between the brothers. In light of the traditional Japanese emphasis on family solidarity and harmony, on the prerogatives of elder brothers over younger brothers, and, at least ideally, on the submissive attitudes of younger toward older persons, somewhat greater emphasis on these points might have been expected. Relative to Americans, the Japanese do give some emphasis to items of this sort, however, for example, the girl's failure to love the elder brother and the elder brother's fury at the younger's refusal to give her up, as well as the elder's statement: "I am the one to marry her." We conclude that the Japanese show, in these respects, no striking departures from the anticipated.

Recall of the emotional and moral aspects of the story coincides with culturally plausible expectations. The Americans tend to lead in recall of items having to do with love (except the item noted above, "The girl did not love the elder brother"). The Japanese tend to lead in items having to do with sadness. The Americans lead in recall

125

of the moral judgment item, containing reference to the elder brother's "evil deed."

This study points up the difficulties inherent in analyzing and interpreting data collected by the story-recall method, and provides a basis for refinement of both the data-gathering device and the analytic categories. But the investigation supports Kroeber's and Nadel's views concerning the potentialities of the study of conceptualizing habits and the usefulness of the type of approach developed by Nadel. Differences in the conceptualizing habits modal among bearers of Japanese and of American cultures have been shown to be inferable from the story-recall data.[40]

Our evidence, drawn from many sources, clearly contradicts those students of child development who have held long and tenaciously to theories that allow no place in early childhood for significant cognitive activity. The observation of children in natural, rather than in experimental, situations, provides impressive evidence of their cognitive capacities and activities.

Available cross-cultural data show, in the cultures of childhood, concepts and knowledge related to both the physical world and the social realm. The specific content of these concept-knowledge systems varies widely from culture to culture. So do the patterns affecting the building of these systems in the minds of children— the extent to which adults customarily answer children's questions, for example, or otherwise encourage the universal inclinations of children toward "curiosity-investigatory" behavior (Harlow) and selective attention to what is novel or surprising. Reasoning about perplexing questions appears in very young children but is predictably more complex in older ones.

Cognitive patterns in a culture of childhood are affected by language and by the focii of interest patterned among adults in a society. Mead has called attention to the relation between language and children's categories of "sense experience," particularly their responses to music, and their color perceptions. She notes too that some children (Manus, for example) do not ask "why" questions; the culture borne by the adults of their society lacks a focus of interest on origins and causalities. Whatever the focii of the adult society— subsistence techniques, law, dancing, oratory—these salient interests will be reflected in the concept-knowledge systems of the society's children and their culture.

The cross-cultural record presents evidence of marked sex differences in concept-knowledge, systems, differences that appear in early childhood and become greater with age. In its cognitive aspects the culture of childhood is ordinarily richer among boys than among girls. In most traditional societies the latter receive little or no instruction or encouragement toward the more intellectually demanding activities and accomplishments.

There is evidence that a culture of childhood will include at least rudiments of the world view characteristic of the adult society. Life is precarious and hard, witchcraft is one of life's hazards, the Thunder Spirits will pity those who plead to them, each boy can and should find his own guardian spirit; these are world-view elements familiar to children in different American Indian societies. Concepts of the supernatural, of a "divine presence" (Jones) for example, are commonplace among children of our own and other complex societies. But such concepts are reflections from the cultures of adults. Contrary to widespread belief, animism is not a childlike mode of conceptualization.

It is clear that the cross-cultural data are sufficient to point up widely held fallacies in assumptions about the capacities and inclinations of children. However, the data are at many points still too scanty to allow for firm definition of the range of child capacities or of the relationship between specific capacities and specifics of the cultures of childhood in which they appear.

NOTES

[1] William Fowler, "Cognitive Learning in Infancy and Early Childhood," *Psychological Bulletin,* 59 (1962), 139.

[2] Harry F. Harlow, "Mice, Monkeys, Men, and Motives," *Psychological Review,* 60 (1953), 28 f.

[3] Barbara Biber et al., *Child Life in School* (New York: E. P. Dutton & Co., 1942), pp. 129 f.

[4] Susan Isaacs, *Intellectual Growth in Young Children* (New York: Schocken Books, 1966).

[5] Fowler, *loc. cit.*

[6] Irving E. Sigel, "The Attainment of Concepts," in Martin L. Hoffman and Lois W. Hoffman, eds., *Review of Child Development Research* (New York: Russell Sage Foundation, 1964), I, 209-248.

[7] William E. Martin, "Rediscovering the Mind of the Child: A Significant Trend in Research in Child Development," *Merrill-Palmer Quarterly of Behavior and Development,* 6 (1959-60), 75.

[8] Sigel, "The Attainment of Concepts," *op. cit.,* p. 209.

[9] Jean Piaget, "Nécessité et Signification des Recherches comparatives en Psychologie génétique," *International Journal of Psychology,* 1 (1966), 3-13.

[10] D. E. Berlyne and Frances D. Frommer, "Some Determinants of the Evidence and Content of Children's Questions," *Child Development,* 37 (1966), 177-188.

[11] *Ibid.,* p. 178.

[12] Isaacs, *op. cit.,* p. 84 (italics original).

[13] Dudley Kidd, *Savage Childhood* (London: Adam and Charles Black, 1906), pp. 76 f.

[14] Wayne Dennis, "Use of Common Objects as Indicators of Cultural Orientations," *Journal of Abnormal and Social Psychology,* 55 (1957), 21-28.

[15] Norman E. Freeberg and Donald T. Payne, "Parental Influence on Cognitive Development in Early Childhood: A Review," *Child Development,* 38 (1967), 81.

[16] Gerald S. Lesser, Gordon Fifer, and Donald H. Clark, "Mental Abilities of Children from Different Social-Class and Cultural Groups," *Monographs of the Society for Research in Child Development,* 30 (1965), 82.

[17] Isaacs, *op. cit.,* pp. 80 f.

[18] *Ibid.,* pp. 81 f.

[19] *Ibid.,* p. 84.

[20] *Ibid.,* p. 84.

[21] Margaret Mead, "The Primitive Child," in Carl Murchison, ed., *A Handbook*

of Child Psychology (Worcester, Mass.: Clark University Press, 1931), p. 683.

[22] *Ibid.*, p. 684.

[23] Margaret Mead, *Children of Their Fathers—Growing Up Among the Ngoni of Malawi* (New York: Holt, Rinehart & Winston, 1968), pp. 42 f.

[24] *Ibid.*, p. 43.

[25] Sister M. Inez Hilger, *Araucanian Child Life and Its Cultural Background,* (Washington, D.C.: Smithsonian Miscellaneous Collections, 133 (1957), pp. 81 f.

[26] D. B. Shimkin, *Childhood and Development Among the Wind River Shoshone* (Berkeley: University of California Press, Anthropological Records, 5 (1947), p. 313.

[27] Fred Kniffen et al., "Walapai Ethnography," *Memoirs of the American Anthropological Association,* 42 (1935), 205 f.

[28] Dorothea Leighton and Clyde Kluckhohn, *Children of the People* (Cambridge, Mass.: Harvard University Press, 1947), p. 39.

[29] *Ibid.*, p. 40.

[30] Nancy O. Lurie, ed., *Mountain Wolf Woman* (Ann Arbor: University of Michigan Press paperback, 1966), pp. 20 f.

[31] *Ibid.*, p. 21.

[32] Rufus M. Jones, *A Small Town Boy* (New York: The Macmillan Company, 1941).

[33] Margaret Mead, *Growing Up in New Guinea* (New York: New American Library, Mentor Book, 1953), pp. 83 f.

[34] *Ibid.*, p. 83.

[35] J. Milton Singer, in Harry Hoijer, ed., "Language in Culture," *American Anthropological Association Memoir* No. 79 (1954), p. 185.

[36] Victor Barnouw, "Acculturation and Personality Among the Wisconsin Chippewa," *American Anthropological Association Memoir* No. 72 (1950), p. 20.

[37] *Anthropology* (New York: Harcourt, Brace & Co., 1948), pp. 604-606.

[38] S. F. Nadel, "Experiments on Cultural Psychology," *Africa,* 10 (1937), 421-435; "A Field Experiment in Racial Psychology," *British Journal of Psychology,* 28 (1937-38), 195-211.

[39] Mary Ellen Goodman, "Culture and Conceptualization: A Study of Japanese and American Children," *Ethnology,* 1 (1962), 374-386.

[40] *Ibid.*, pp. 383 f.

8

Play, Games, and Humor

"At home we always had to keep playing
all the time. Here we can learn real letters
and numbers and things" (American five-
year-old's reaction to a French village
school).

L. Wylie

Writers familiar only with children in Western-urban societies tend
to assume that in all of the cultures of childhood there is a sharp
work/play dichotomy. They assume too that all children recoil from
work and wish only to play endlessly. But anthropological reports
provide ample evidence that these assumptions are by no means justified.

In many societies children simply do not make a sharp distinction between work and play. In their report on Navaho children
Leighton and Kluckhohn comment:

"Play" becomes "work" at times and vice versa. Thus, while the little shepherd works by taking the sheep out in the morning, he spends considerable
periods of the time while watching them graze in playing with them or the
dog or his fellow shepherd or the sticks and rocks around.[1]

Arab shepherd boys, whose favorite "plaything" is a slingshot
(usually made by each boy for himself), use it also as a principal
"tool" in herding. If a sheep wanders too far from the flock, the
young shepherd will skillfully fire a stone so that it falls just in
front of the animal and makes it turn. [2]

Evaluating Work and Play

To the extent that children do differentiate between work and play, the former may be at least as highly valued.

Among boys of five Indian tribes "work appears as a 'good thing to do,' and not to work or to neglect one's work as a 'bad thing to do.'" Fifty per cent of the responses were of this order, while among white children there were only 10 to 20 per cent of such responses. Leighton and Kluckhohn add, concerning the Navaho who figured in this study:

It is a question of attached values. . . . The Navaho [child] expects to work . . . The white child expects to play. . . . If he [white] is asked to do some work, he feels that his playing time is being taken from him, whereas the Navaho child feels that he is being given an opportunity to participate in the family activity.[3]

A sharp contrast of culturally patterned values has been highlighted also by Wayne Dennis in his comparative study of American and Lebanese children of the same age range (five to eleven years). All the subjects were living in Beirut. Dennis concludes: "Lebanese responses seem to indicate that industriousness is highly valued." For these children "much of the world seems to be oriented toward utilitarian ends."[4] They seldom mentioned play, and they made no reference to art, music, athletics, or sensory pleasures other than eating. But the Beirut colony of American children, whose families are quite comparable in social class to those of the Lebanese subjects, give very different responses. They show great concern with play. "In contrast with the seriousness of the Lebanese children, life for the American children in Beirut would seem to constitute a perpetual vacation."[5]

Few societies can afford the luxury of allowing their children to enjoy anything even approximating a "perpetual vacation." Among tribal peoples this luxury can be indulged only where nature is unusually beneficent. Truk, in the Caroline Islands, is one of these favored spots. Fischer reports:

. . . nature is fairly kind in Truk and children have traditionally been allowed to spend their time playing, with few demands on them for concentrated effort in subsistence labor or otherwise. Serious applied effort, physical or intellectual, is hardly expected of people until middle age.[6]

Preferred Types of Play

Types of play preferred in early childhood appear to be rather less culturally variable than work/play concepts and attitudes. Certainly one type of play—mimicry—is universal, and particularly the mimicking of adult activities. In such dramatic play children practice before one another the roles they will someday play as hunters, warriors, gardeners, mothers, or whatever else the world of their adults shows as expected and proper activities of men and women. Through observation and imitation of that world, the culture of childhood comes to include versions of adult values as well as of adult roles. Certain of the roles, those sensed to be especially significant or interesting, are likely to be played with great frequency (cops and robbers, cowboys and Indians, for example). The values these roles convey—excitement, violence, certain skills—are reinforced in the culture of childhood as the roles are observed and practiced.

In a Mexican village studied by Michael Maccoby and his research colleagues, "dramatic play or mimicry most characterizes the play of the children under 8." Little girls imitate the baby care and household activities of grown women. Little boys imitate the behavior of men, especially those activities of the more dramatic sorts, such as pistol waving and drunkenness. Games of skill and competition (for example, marbles and penny-pitching) are played increasingly from the age of four, and largely by boys.[7]

The toys available to children may be many or few, depending in part on environmental resources and in part on the traditional patterns of each culture of childhood. The interlocking of these two factors is vividly illustrated in reports on the toys customary to the Chama and Guarayu children of the Bolivian jungles.

The Chama children spend many hours creatively shaping toys . . . from jungle raw materials. . . . Pet birds . . . and monkeys . . . also occupy their attention.

Papaya . . . and banana . . . leaves are used for umbrellas . . . and play house . . . roofs. . . . Large soft leaves . . . are used as toy cups; . . . these may also be pressed against the teeth and popped . . . like bubble gum. Juice from the *kwasoxa* tree is blown . . . into durable "soap" bubbles. . . . Small reeds . . . are cut in differing lengths and lit on one side to make variously toned whistles. . . .[8]

The readily available jungle materials are utilized by the Chama children in many other ways as well. Little children string colored seeds, alligator teeth, and small shells for bracelets, model in clay, make shuttlecock and balloon-like toys. Older boys whittle balsa wood, carve hard lumps of clay, and create in these and other ways a great variety of models (such as airplanes and canoes) and toys

133

(such as whistling tops, slingshots, and a reed "gun").[9] Among the Bolivian Guarayu children, who live in a similar jungle environment, the cultural patterns for utilizing local materials are equally many and perhaps even more varied. These children make kites, stilts, marbles, and even "bouncing balls." These balls are made "by winding long strings of crude rubber into a round shape."[10]

Play Technology

In cultures like these (Chama and Guarayu), and in the frontier and early rural phases of American culture, commercially made playthings were seldom available. But the play patterns of the young were not impoverished as a result. On the contrary, they incorporated a great deal of what might be called "play technology"—of know-how with respect to the materials, the fashioning, and the use of environmental resources. This aspect of the culture of childhood, like other aspects, was transmitted to children by both adults and older children. In small, close-knit communities the process of transmission was a natural expression of that closeness and a reinforcement of it. With the nearly complete commercialization of toys and games, as in today's great urban-industrial centers around the world, the "generation gap" is seldom bridged by the hours and attention required for the transmission of play technology.

Cross-Cultural Similarities

However, despite this and many other contrasts between traditional and modern societies, some similarities survive. In almost all societies the play patterns of boys and girls become increasingly separated and differentiated as the children grow older. Moreover, "boys engage in formal games far more frequently than girls, and many games are not played at all by girls."[11] This statement refers specifically to the Mexican village of Tzintzuntzan, but it would hold true for a large majority of the cultures of childhood.

By the age of 8, except for games played within the schoolyard (generally tag or volleyball), girls and boys neither play together nor play the same games.[12]

Similar patterns are reported for the Chippewa Indians:

While small they played with toys made by their elders: when a little older, boys and girls played together in games and in imitation of elders; when

134

still older sexes excluded each other and played apart and tolerated no inter-ference from each other....[13]

There are, however, societies in which boys and girls from about six meet occasionally to play at being married, at keeping house, and looking after their children. In his autobiography a Kwakiutl Indian recalls playing "pretend to have wives" until he was twelve. He says: "I remember that we see our parents and my brother what they do—how they sleep together, eat together, all those things, and we try to do them too."[14]

Play, Games, and Adult Roles

The cultures of childhood vary widely with respect to range and richness of play materials and with respect to those formalized play patterns which belong to the "game" category. Boys' games are generally more numerous and more strenuous than girls' games. And of boys' games a significant proportion are likely to be unmistakably related to the roles of the adult male. Apache Indian culture was notably rich in such games, all of them demanding and some highly dangerous. Morris Opler comments:

Many of the pastimes for boys are in reality mock battles and are a definite part of the training and hardening process through which the youths are passing. Often the boys themselves organize these games, but frequently the adults suggest or arrange them.[15]

Athletic competitions—particularly foot races, riding, and swimming contests—serve the same need for "training and harden-ing" the young. Among the Apache such contests are organized for girls as well as for boys, and sometimes for the sexes together. Both boys and girls are given unusually thorough and careful preparation for the survival needs of adulthood. Much of this preparation is in the guise of games and sports.

Under the influence of modern Western culture these tradition-al patterns are very likely to disappear. Of the native peoples of New Zealand it is reported:

... traditional Maori games which once filled the days of the children and the evenings of the older youth are no longer played. Many of these games prepared for war, and many for fowling and fishing. Others allowed com-petition on a scale of limited violence in the use of a number of small skills, and a few symbolized and perhaps initiated courtship....

Yet not all of the aims of . . . life are serious even today; recreation

135

takes an important place, as spontaneous amusement or in an organized form [such as dancing, singing, sports].[16]

Modern urban emphasis on games and sports is at least as heavy as in any tribal or transitional society, but its objectives are fitness—fitness both physical and social—rather than survival. The modern Western point of view is stated succinctly by British psychologist J. A. Hadfield, who urges "natural sports" (sailing, mountain climbing, swimming, and so on) because "the very fact that the boy is up against the forces of nature brings out his hardihood and makes a man of him. Facing a common danger also brings out cooperation, comradeship, leadership, and the team spirit. . . ." But Hadfield applauds also games, because they require acceptance of rules. Therefore, "they are a good training in citizenship. . . . Games can develop qualities of character and social consideration of others. . . . [They] should therefore be an *essential* part of school life."[17] Hadfield's views are by no means novel; philosopher Karl Groos, writing at the turn of the century on *The Play of Man*, advanced similar arguments.[18]

Motivations for Play, Games, and Humor

This kind of modern rationale has been somewhat superseded by points of view tracing ultimately to Freud and the Freudians. In their conceptual framework play, games, and humor as well are seen as symbolic expressions of either "racial" or individual psychic problems. Here is a representative statement:

Being able to joke is a uniquely human resource which the young child seizes upon in order to transform his painful feelings into pleasure and thus gain the gratification denied him at every turn by parents and environment. His problems are the substance of his humor. . . . Word-play, one of the earliest forms of children's humor, shows that children use ambiguity and the magic power of words . . . to change their own identities, even to drop for a moment the burden of being a child.[19]

Interpretations of these sorts remain highly speculative, unproved, and quite probably unprovable. On the other hand the linkage between play, games, and both survival and fitness is clear cut and widely documented.

It is equally clear and unarguable that in all societies the cultures of childhood include something—little or much—that is simply "for fun." The fun may be solitary and quiet or gregarious and noisy, brain teasing or horseplay, harsh and competitive, or gentle but provocative. Patterns vary widely and they have been studied but little.

Children perceive much that is funny, but researchers study them grimly, and almost completely miss the fun. The index to a recent *Review of Child Development Research*—two thick volumes —contains not one single reference to humor.[20] Each of two major works on the sociology of childhood completely lacks index references to humor![21] For a 650-page book reporting the details of child behavior in school the index carries eleven references to hostility and one to humor.[22] Such imbalances tell us more about the perceptual systems of the researchers than of the children they study.

Cultures, of course, differ in their definitions of humor. It may be, moreover, that what the young child finds funny is generally a matter more of the comic than the humorous. The distinction between the two is made neatly by Gordon Allport:

[Humor] is the ability to laugh at the things one loves (including, of course, oneself and all that pertains to oneself), and still to love them. . . . The sense of humor must be distinguished sharply from the cruder sense of the comic. . . . A young child has a keen sense of the comic [which consists usually of absurdities, horseplay, puns] but seldom if ever laughs at himself.[23]

Toddlers sometimes babble nonsense sounds "partly for the sheer pleasure of hearing the sound patterns come out but partly also in a spirit of deliberate silliness, as though recognizing the absurdity. . . ." In children of preschool age language command is such that "sense and nonsense are consciously intermingled."[24]

The playful and imaginative use of a language, whatever the nature of that language, is no doubt culturally conditioned too. It may be invited, encouraged, rewarded, or not. But Soviet author Kornei Chukovsky—who is perhaps the dean of children's poets and a serious student of early childhood as well, believes that all children are naturally inclined to play with words. He cites pages of delightful examples, for instance:

"Where did you put the broom?" the mother asked the boy. "Over there, on the stair," he pointed. And no sooner did he utter the words than he noticed that there was rhythm and rhyme in them, and he began to chant:
    "Over there—
    On the stair.
    Over there—
    On the stair."

... And this is what three-and-a-half year old Tania did with the word milk:

Ilk, silk, tilk
I eat kasha with milk.
Ilks, silks, tilks
I eat kashas with milks.

Chukovsky believes that "in the beginning of our childhood we are all 'versifiers.' "[25]

Perhaps we are, but very likely there are already great differences—individual differences and cultural differences as well—with respect to versifying skills. Certainly storytelling abilities and inclinations vary widely as between individual nursery school children. This fact was evident in the more than 500 stories that were collected at the Gesell Institute Nursery School between 1955 and 1961. Age and sex difference were as apparent as might be expected; five-year-olds tell longer stories than do two- or three-year-olds, "girls tell longer stories than do boys; . . . girls are more concerned with morality; . . ." "girls' stories generally are more realistic and closer to home than those of boys," and girls more often mention their mothers. However, boys more than girls picture mother as friendly; "girls see fathers in a more favorable light than do boys."[26]

Some of us seem to be from the beginning jokesters. There is without doubt a wide range of individual variation in talent and inclination toward joking as well as toward versifying and storytelling. Chukovsky no doubt overstates his case, and ignores cultural differences, when he asserts that we are all "versifiers" in early childhood. Without going so far in making parallel assertions about the young child as humorist, one can still make a case for him as inclined to perceive in the world around him what seems to him funny, and even to make deliberate attempts at contributing to its funniness. Indeed, Chukovsky's own charming collection of children's versifications is full of intended humor, and all parents and teachers of young children can cite—and parents will do so without invitation —dozens of illustrations.

Perceptions and productions of absurdities in language are sometimes paralleled in the playing out of absurdities in social roles. An observer at the Vassar College nursery school preserved this extraordinarily fine example. Four-year-old-boys were overheard caricaturing adult women, and "convulsed by their own wit" meanwhile:

Jack: It's *lovely* to see you!
Danny: I'm so happy to see you!
Jack: How *are* you? How have you *been*?
Danny: Sorry I have to go so quick.

Jack: (adding broad strokes of four-year-old slapstick humor) I hope you have a good time falling down and bumping your head.[27]

Jack and Danny demonstrate a sense of the comic at a level rather sophisticated for four-year-olds. Among young American children the "horseplay" level predominates; pretended mutilations are likely to be thought very funny, and scatological references as well.[28] Puns, wisecracking, telling jokes—these comic forms are common among school age children but not among younger ones.

The crudities of what young children find comic are of a piece with their cruel tendencies. Sympathy is certainly not beyond the capacities of preschool children. However, a toddler's apparently sympathetic act toward another child may be "less from a feeling of compassion than from an inability to distinguish the other child's emotions from his own." But a preschool child's behavior toward someone who has been hurt or scolded, particularly if it is another child, may be "akin to mature sympathy."[29]

. . . The preschool child's feelings of sympathy develop from direct participation in what happens to other children into a more mature sympathy based on a detached understanding.

. . . The feeling of adults present a much greater problem [for understanding, than those of other children]. To the preschool child, adults—even when he consciously or unconsciously mocks their ways—appear as omniscient, omnipotent beings who order other people and things around and do only what they want to do.[30]

These several examples demonstrate that a dichotomy between work and play, and a strong preference for the latter, is by no means a universal feature of the cultures of childhood. Navaho children regard work as "an opportunity to participate in the family activity."[31] Lebanese children value industriousness and exhibit a seriousness quite unlike the attitudes of a group of American children studied for comparison.

With respect to preferred types of play there is greater cross-cultural similarity. Dramatic play and mimicking adult activities are commonplace favorites among young children, and games of skill and competition are almost universally popular with older boys.

In societies isolated from commercial sources toys are made from locally available materials. The "play technology" required is a significant feature of the cultures of childhood. Its transmission, by adults and by older to younger children, functions to bridge age differences and increase solidarity between age groups.

Observations in many societies show that play patterns of girls and boys diverge as they become older. Ordinarily, older boys and girls neither share play nor play patterns. Boys' games are generally the more numerous and strenuous. In traditional societies much play was, in fact, a "training and hardening" of the boys[32] in preparation for their adult roles. In modern societies too this concept has been prevalent; the celebrated "playing fields of Eton" were long credited for their place in the training of England's leaders. In complex societies the emphasis now seems to be on the importance of sports and games for physical fitness and for "fun."

There can be no doubt that play and games function to promote both training and fitness, but their functions include also their fun and pleasure. Probably all the cultures of childhood include something—little or much—that is merely "for fun." Fun is to some extent culturally defined, and children's concepts of humor have been little studied. In Western cultures (American and Russian) there is ample evidence that many children of preschool age play with language for humorous effects, and mimic what they perceive as funny in adult behavior. It is reasonable to suppose that these and such other familiar patterns of child humor as practical jokes are cross-culturally widespread, if not universal.

NOTES

[1] Dorothea Leighton and Clyde Kluckhohn, *Children of the People* (Cambridge, Mass.: Harvard University Press, 1947), p. 169.

[2] Hilma Granquist, *Birth and Childhood Among the Arabs* (Helsingfors, Finland: Soderstrom and Company, 1947), pp. 127 f.

[3] Leighton and Kluckhohn, *op. cit.*, p. 169.

[4] Wayne Dennis, "Uses of Common Objects as Indicators of Cultural Orientations," *Journal of Abnormal and Social Psychology*, 55 (1957), 27.

[5] *Ibid.*, p. 28.

[6] John L. Fischer, "Schools for the Natives of Truk, Caroline Islands," *Human Organization*, 20 (1961), 86.

[7] Michael Maccoby, Nancy Modiano, and Patricia Lander, "Games and Social Character in a Mexican Village," *Psychiatry*, 27 (1964), 153 f.

[8] Nola Shoemaker, "Toys of Chama (Eseejja) Indian Children," *American Anthropologist*, 66 (1964), 1152.

[9] *Ibid.*, p. 1152.

[10] Evangelyn Jackson, "Native Toys of the Guarayu Indians," *American Anthropologist*, 66 (1964), 1154.

[11] George M. Foster, *Empire's Children: The People of Tzintzuntzan* (Washington, D.C.: Smithsonian Institution, 1948), p. 238.

[12] Maccoby et al., "Games and Social Character in a Mexican Village," *op. cit.*, p. 154.

[13] Sister M. Inez Hilger, *Chippewa Child Life and Its Cultural Background* (Washington, D.C.: Smithsonian Institution, 1948), p. 238.

[14] Clellan S. Ford, *Smoke from Their Fires: The Life of a Kwakiutl Chief* (New Haven: Yale University Press, 1941), pp. 68 f.

[15] Morris E. Opler, *Childhood and Youth in Jicarilla Apache Society* (Los Angeles: The Southwest Museum, 1946), p. 76.

[16] H. B. Hawthorn, "The Maori: A Study in Acculturation," *American Anthropological Association Memoir* No. 64 (1944), p. 34.

[17] J. A. Hadfield, *Childhood and Adolescence* (Baltimore: Penguin Books, 1962), pp. 175 f.

[18] Karl Groos, *The Play of Man*, trans. Elizabeth L. Baldwin (New York: D. Appleton and Co., 1914).

[19] Toby Talbot, ed., *The World of the Child* (Garden City, N.Y.: Doubleday & Co., Inc., 1967), p. 273.

[20] Lois W. Hoffman and Martin L. Hoffman, eds., *Review of Child Development Research* (New York: Russell Sage Foundation, 1966).

[21] Oscar W. Ritchie and Marvin R. Koller, *Sociology of Childhood* (New York: Appleton-Century-Crofts, 1964); James H. S. Bossard and Eleanor Sto-

ker Ball, *The Sociology of Child Development,* 3d ed. (New York: Harper and Brothers, 1960).

[22] Barbara Biber et al., *Child Life in School* (New York: E. P. Dutton & Co., 1942).

[23] Gordon W. Allport, *Pattern and Growth in Personality* (New York: Holt, Rinehart & Winston, 1961), pp. 292 f.

[24] L. Joseph Stone and Joseph Church, *Childhood and Adolescence* (New York: Random House, 1957), p. 126.

[25] Kornei Chukovsky, *From Two to Five,* ed. and trans. Miriam Morton (Berkeley and Los Angeles: University of California Press, 1963), pp. 62 f.

[26] Louise Bates Ames, "Children's Stories," *Genetic Psychology Monographs,* 73 (1966), 394.

[27] Stone and Church, *op. cit.,* p. 153.

[28] *Ibid.,* p. 149.

[29] *Ibid.,* p. 147.

[30] *Ibid.,* p. 160.

[31] Leighton and Kluckhohn, *op. cit.,* p. 169.

[32] Opler, *op. cit.,* p. 79.

9

The End of Childhood

Treat your son as a rajah until he is five, as
a slave until he is fifteen, and then as a
friend.

Mainpuri Indian saying

Among many peoples the culturally patterned views of childhood
incorporate age/stage concepts as definitive as those expressed in the
Mainpuri saying just above. In earlier chapters we have noted this
fact, along with examples that illustrate a wide range of variation
in age/stage expectations in the cultures of childhood and in the
wider cultures as well. Anthropologists know too that there is great
variation with respect to concepts concerning the end of childhood—
whether, when, and how it is defined and marked.

Childhood as Transition

Such variations notwithstanding, anthropologist Solon T. Kimball suggests that all of childhood, "in its several stages and on to the
adult world," can be viewed as a transition. And he adds: "In our culture, at least, each child is anxious to move through [childhood].
Adults are the ones who show nostalgia."[1]

Certainly our child- and youth-centered culture presents just
such a paradox; children are impatient to complete the transition to
adulthood (under-thirty adulthood, to be sure!) while adults (over-
thirty adults mainly) show nostalgia and an inclination to cling to
whatever signs of youthfulness they can preserve or simulate. Both
the young and their elders romanticize what is not theirs—on the one
hand, the fancied omnipotence of elders, and on the other, childhood and youth remembered as an idyll of carefree fun, or a rea-

143

sonable approximation thereof. But however unreal the expectations of children or the recollections of adults, to the detached observer all of childhood does indeed present the features of a transition.

In earlier chapters we noted salient aspects of the manifold cultural phrasings of this fact. We at least illustrated significant aspects of the dawning—the period in which each child acquires certain fundamentals of that culture of childhood to which he is heir by virtue of membership in a particular society, perhaps a subsociety as well. We have explored in some depth certain major segments of the cultures of childhood, segments that seem to appear in one or another guise or degree in all of them. The treatment is far from exhaustive, but I believe it touches upon what is essential to the cultures of childhood and to the transition from infancy to adolescence. What remains is to note, at least briefly, something of the variety of rites by which the end of childhood is culturally marked, and something of the cultural phrasings of adolescence.

The Nature of "the Adolescent"

American "experts" on adolescence have been mainly psychologists unfamiliar with cross-cultural data. The result is exactly what we have had occasion repeatedly to note and deplore—generalizations based on one society, usually the United States, or even on a limited time/social space segment of United States culture, but stated as though they applied always and everywhere. The pages of a highly respected publication *(Review of Child Development Research)* provide an example of such culture-bound pronouncements:

The adolescent is propelled into friendship by the psychic conflicts of his age and by the ego task he faces. He must detach his impulse life from the family; he needs a new authority to substitute for parental authority as he works through individuated inner controls. . . . He needs friends desperately. . . . Theoretically at least, adolescents cleave to peer-group norms as though any deviation—in dress or attitude or behavior—somehow threatened the inner integrity.[2]

The statement is made up of a series of assumptions about "the adolescent." Any one of these implications of universality can be demolished in a moment by any competent anthropologist. He can cite at once half a dozen exceptions—societies in which adolescents do not behave in accord with these assumptions. And careful observers of our own and of other "advanced" societies also can offer impressive evidence of individual and subgroup exceptions to these sweeping generalizations.

144

The Biocultural Mix

Cultural pressures toward dignity, conformity, and conservatism will, in most cases, go far to produce adolescents who are on the average dignified, conforming, and conservative (as their culture defines those qualities). But their behavior will be the expression of a biocultural mix, on the "bio-" side of which these charateristics will be conspicuous: (1) physical energy at a new high for the individual, and possibly at an all-time high in relation to his life span; (2) psychic energy at a similar high, and seeking outlets in what our society knows as "kicks"; (3) a new high in awareness of the self as standing on a threshold, of approaching or having just reached the point of being tried and tested in the adult world. The combination of these "highs" goes far to explain what is cross-culturally apparent in the young and what the not-so-young can easily recall: a restlessness, an erratic emotional pattern, a thrill in trying oneself at something new, and especially something believed to be at least a little dangerous or daring.

The extent to which specific cultures and subcultures enhance, contain, control, or direct these "bio-" factors is enormously variable. There is probably no culture lacking at least some relevant patterns. Girls and boys are almost sure to be treated differently; the beginning and the end of a period comparable to what we call adolescence will be more or less marked; the very existence of such a period, and the cultural expectations regarding it, are variable from almost nil to our own extremes of permissiveness, anxiety, and attentiveness.

The Gradualist Pattern

Prominent among culturally patterned concepts is what has been called the "gradualist" view; it coincides with Kimball's concept of all childhood as a transition toward adulthood. Edward Norbeck and his research colleagues have identified a number of cultures in which this is the patterned outlook. Individual differences are expected, but ordinarily no abrupt changes are anticipated. The norm is a gradual transition from infancy to maturity (a transition that may extend even into the mid-thirties).[3] The Cheyenne Indian view, as reported by Hoebel, is in harmony with this conception:

Children [excluding infants] have the same qualities as adults; they lack only in experience. . . .

Children should, on their level, engage in adult activities. . . .

145

Children become adults as soon as they are physically able to perform adult roles.[4]

The End of Childhood: Ceremonial Markers

In many societies childhood is seen as marked by phases or stages. This fact has been noted and illustrated repeatedly in earlier chapters (especially Chapters 3, 4, and 5). "Ceremonial markers of passage from one social stage to another" are patterned in many cultures.[5] But no passage is so often and significantly marked as that which functions to signal the end of childhood.

Psychologists and anthropologists have vied with one another in producing elaborate, even bizarre, interpretations of "puberty rites." Norbeck et al would seem to have administered to such efforts a *coup de grâce* when they commented: "We do not think we go too far in saying that [J.W.M.] Whiting and his associates overburden us with hypotheses. As their research is presented, it concerns hypothetical conflict that is hypothetically resolved."[6] It seems to me reasonable to conclude:

Transitions from childhood to adolescence and to maturity are in some societies ceremonially marked, though in widely differing ways and degrees. . . .[7]

[Pubertal changes as such] may be scarcely recognized; they may be celebrated before or after the fact, briefly or at length. They may be celebrated with more or less formality, "hazing," . . . or formal instruction. Little or much may be made of physiological maturing . . . [while social maturing may be emphasized].[8]

In view of this diversity the term "puberty rite" is not really appropriate to all of the forms the "ceremonial markers" take. "Initiation rite" too is an inexact phrase suggesting, as it does, hazing and other features widely associated with admission to secret societies. Eisenstadt has attempted to summarize the crucial points and common features between many otherwise diverse rites. He calls attention to the following:

—all these rites function to transform pre-adults into "full adult members of the tribe . . .";
—during the rites the young "are symbolically divested of the characteristics of youth and invested with those of adulthood . . . [by] bodily mutilation, circumcision, taking on of a new name, symbolic rebirth, etc." or by

symbolic separation from childhood associations, especially, in the case of boys, from mothers;

—the rites sometimes dramatize generational differences, but "the basic complementariness . . . is stressed . . .";

—tribal lore is transmitted and the young are harangued and exhorted concerning ideals and values;

—the neophyte adult is invested with new authority, in at least a limited degree.[9]

End-of-childhood rites have captured the attention of scholars in part because in many societies they take extremely dramatic forms. The traditional practices of native Australians are among the most arresting. In these societies small boys were treated gently and even indulgently. But initiation rites (always performed at puberty and sometimes prepubertally as well) brought extraordinary tests and trials.

At initiation new psychic paths are made by isolation, terror, fatigue, pain, mystery, music, drama, grave instruction—means implicitly prescient and in overt use a memorable spectacle. . . .

Durmugam [subject of a life history] was initiated . . . at a time (about 1913) when a relatively large number of aborigines could be assembled and the full panoply of ceremonial forms could be followed. He emerged a blackfellow for life. He did not simply reach manhood; he was *given* it, was *made* a man by men who stood for and taught him to stand for a tradition. . . .

The initiations teach boys to be men; to know pain and ignore it; to feel fear and master it; to want, but to bear the necessary costs; to grasp that outside society they are nothing (in the isolation of initiation they are called "wild dogs") and, inside it, the masters . . . The vital impulses are not crushed, but steered . . . [10]

In New Guinea, as in Australia, traditional initiations are harsh. Watson, in his life history of an Agarabi of the New Guinea Highlands, provides a vivid glimpse of the ceremonies:

In telling of his initiation, Bantao insisted that he faced the prospect with fears no greater than the rest of his age group. The basic purpose of this painful ceremony, performed jointly for all boys of a certain age, is to assert their masculinity and their manly duties by putting them to a series of cruel tests. The ceremony is also the occasion for severing the boys from their lives as children and from nearly every aspect of the women's sphere. They are admitted into residence in the men's house, a stage that marks the beginning of several years of constant but less formal indoctrination. Formerly iyampo, they now become pumara, and will be shown the

147

sacred flutes and the bullroarer. They discover closely guarded male secrets such as cane swallowing in which a length of flexible rattan is passed through the mouth to the somach and then extracted again.[11]

"The bloody rites of the initiation itself" include a mock (but by no means painless) battle between the men and initiates, the bleeding of each boy's nose with coarse grass, the cutting of the glans penis with a bamboo sliver, and the pushing of stinging nettles up the urethra. Once recovered from these ordeals the boy begins to savor the benefits of his new status: "After initiation the youths become increasingly involved in courtship and formalized sex play, generally with a series of girls. This continues until marriage and the birth of one's children when manhood really begins."[12]

Differences in Ceremonial Markers and in Sex Behavior Expectations for Boys and Girls

Among tribal peoples boys' initiations are seldom so formidable as these. For girls, ceremonies of any sort at all are much less frequent and never so harsh. With the exception of clitoridectomy (a rarely occurring parallel to circumcision or to cutting of the glans penis) society ordinarily requires little to mark a girl's entrance into womanhood. At her first menses, perhaps at subsequent menstruations as well, it may be required that she isolate herself in a menstrual hut. During menstruation she may be required to observe certain taboos with respect to her own activities, to the handling of household implements, or with respect to adult males. Ordinarily, a girl's physical and social maturing are to the people of her society of relatively little moment as compared with a boy's. Either or both may be essentially ignored, however.

Arapaho [Indians] had no prepuberty fasts nor puberty rites for either girls or boys. Young men were allowed to fast after they had given evidence of mature judgment. This rarely happened while they were in their teens.[13]

Among "The Fierce People" (the Yanomamö Indians of Venezuela and Brazil) there is no ceremony marking manhood. Girls, on the other hand, receive special and ceremonious treatment at their first menses (mainly a matter of confinement for a week, after which "a girl is eligible to begin life as a wife and take up residence with her husband").[14]

The "double standard" occurs in many societies. Geertz reports

148

of Java, for example, that once a girl has passed puberty her parents are increasingly uneasy lest she become pregnant before marriage. Their concern is less a matter of morality than of practicality. Once she is pregnant it becomes "difficult to marry her off and the father may have to pay the groom to marry her . . . Boys, on the other hand, are allowed complete freedom. By the time they are married they are expected to be sexually experienced."[15]

In more complex cultures such as that of the United States, the sexual double standard has become almost an anachronism. Traces of double standards of other sorts still prevail, however. The parents of a middle-class girl who drops out of college, even high school, are likely to be less concerned than the parents of a boy. These attitudes are realistic; few girls will support themselves, much less take on dependents. Conversely, few boys will fail to do so. There can be no question which sex most needs the maximum possible education.

It seems likely that young people are themselves quite realistic and quite undisturbed about this aspect of the double standard. A recent large-scale study in Australia leads to this conclusion:

The characteristic male adolescent . . . seems to envisage himself as a future citizen with family responsibilities . . . [He] appears to adopt the traditional male-role from an early age. . . .

The characteristic female adolescent . . . is fairly well-equipped to undertake responsibilities usually associated with the male role, [but] she receives, and expects, a greater measure of protection within her family. She is more concerned than the male with domestic tasks and social obligations.[16]

In the United States a similar study would produce similar findings. American girls are less career-oriented than were their mothers and grandmothers. Complaints about double standards are seldom heard from young women in the United States.

Ceremonial Markers in Complex Cultures

In complex cultures there are no precise equivalents of tribal puberty or initiation rites. The very complexity of the culture is a partial explanation.

The simple ceremony of the tribal culture is likely to be paralleled in the complex culture by several ceremonies each related to a different activity system. That is: in place of one ceremony that marks adulthood as such, there may be ceremonies marking adulthood in the religious system (confirmation or Bar Mitzvah, for exam-

149

ple), educational system (graduation), in the sphere of citizenship (army induction), and others. Also, there will most likely be, in each of these systems, a series of ceremonies marking advances through its more or less elaborate status hierarchy. Where the social system is highly differentiated with respect to statuses and functions the simple distinction between adult and preadult is no longer adequate or meaningful. It becomes important to know in which parts of the overall social system the individual now qualifies as mature and the degree of his maturity.

In content as well as in number the ceremonies of complex societies are likely to differ from those of tribal societies. The latter tend to emphasize sex-role esoterica as well as subsistence (for example: hunting, gardening), social, and supernatural knowledge and skills. In complex cultures the content varies widely from one activity system to another, but sex-role esoterica are likely to be minimally represented in any. Subsistence content too is likely to be minimal. Indeed, in complex cultures the ceremonies serve to recognize age, knowledge, and skills already attained rather than as occasions for imparting knowledge and skills.

In large societies whose people are clearly class-stratified, ceremonial markers for lower-class youth are likely to be few and simple as compared with those for upper-middle and upper-class youth. The former, for a variety of reasons, seldom achieve formal maturity in multiple activity systems, if in any. They are unlikely to advance far, if at all, through the status hierarchy of an activity system. They are seldom the beneficiaries of rewards and incentives such as the ceremonial markers undoubtedly and universally provide to hasten and facilitate transitions toward increasing maturity.

In complex societies ceremonial markers are not necessarily public spectacles, trials, or even celebrations. They may function to convey class or family standards and values, and to strengthen the child's awareness of his class and family identity.

In his account of *A Chinese Childhood* (a childhood that must have begun at about the turn of the century) Chiang Yee describes a family ceremony of high personal significance:

On the New Year's Eve of my twelfth year . . . my father called me into his study and sent me to ask my grandfather whether I might be shown the family clan book [an account of the family history]. . . . My grandfather gave his consent . . . my father thought it best to exhibit the clan book in the central hall, where our ancestral shrine stood, so that all members of the household could attend. . . .

It was a memorable evening. All the lanterns in the hall were lit, and my father, after changing his dress and burning incense at the ancestral shrine, climbed up a ladder and took down very respectfully the wooden case in which the clan books were kept. There were thirty or forty volumes. . . .

My father seated himself at the table, with me standing on his right hand and two cousins . . . on his left.[17]

Patterned Expectations
and Parent-Adolescent Relations

In this impressive setting Chiang Yee's father reviewed the history of a family whose origins were documented to the first century B.C. Its heritage of achievement and honor were heavily emphasized, and the maturing children—boys particularly—were made to understand their responsibility for preserving that heritage.

The Chinese, with their ideals of filial piety and reverence to tradition, authority and the past, enjoin their youngsters never to sever relations with their elders. The Americans, with their ideals of freedom, equality, and drive for creativity and for future, encourage their youngsters to be independent of the adults almost from the beginning of life. . . . Independence from parents simply means that they must seek affiliation with peer groups.[18]

The Chinese of whom anthropologist Hsu speaks are still mainly cultural traditionalists, although they live in Hawaii, where (in 1949) he studied their young people. Hsu's comparative data on American adolescents in Chicago show the striking contrast he mentions in the passage just cited, and documents once again that adolescence need not be laden with rebellion and emotionality. He writes:

The most striking difference, in fact, between the Chinese American adolescents in Hawaii and white American adolescents on the mainland is the absence [among the former] of overt rebellion against authority. The "big fight" with parents is lacking. . . . White Americans anticipate more problems as their children approach adolescence; [Chinese parents in Hawaii] . . . expect less and less. . . .[19]

Hsu goes on to evaluate certain large-scale implications of these disparate parental expectations and youth cultures. He notes that the American patterns lead toward personal independence from adults but also toward compensatory dependence on that relatively unreliable resource—the peer group. Peers are fickle in their attachments. They must be constantly wooed. Peer group dependence thereby contributes to the personal insecurity that is one price to be paid for

151

freedom from close family ties. But that freedom, and that critical attitude toward elders and toward tradition which often accom-
panies the freedom, support idealism and reform. "American
youths tend to go out to improve things . . . and to explore unknown
possibilities. This is one of the secrets of strength in American culture."[20]

Intergenerational Discontinuities

In light of the rapid acceleration of youth "rebellion" during
the 1960s (in Communist China as well as in the urban United States
and in many other complex societies), it may be appropriate to raise a
question about this "secret of strength." Is there an optimum point
of intergenerational discontinuity? When that point has been
passed, can this discontinuity become for the society a secret of
weakness rather than of strength? The answers, I think, must be
affirmative in both cases.

Cross-cultural research data point up also a crucial and subtle
aspect of relevant conceptualizing patterns. The studies in question
have examined youth views with respect to the claims of the group
over those of the individual. Comparison of American and German
youth (urban middle class, as of 1946) yielded predictable results, as
did comparisons of anti-Nazi and Nazi youth; the Americans and the
anti-Nazis were found to support individual rights as against group
prerogatives. But when the study was replicated with urban middle-
class Filipino youth, some strikingly different conceptualizing patterns emerged. Stoodley, who conducted the Filipino study, comments:

. . . the Filipino did not see a multi-dimensional situation in the questions
[asked in all the studies], but a uni-dimensional one. Human rights and
group rights were not considered to be in opposition. They were seen as part
of the same "moral" order and had to be related within that order. . . . [Also]
prerogative was not regarded as license or naked power, but as social obligation. Thus, overtones of strength and weakness, domination and submission, were muted or absent.[21] . . . [Filipino youth] see the individual as closely
identified with the group and, as a result, [they] make less distinction between group rights and individual rights than either German or American
youth.[22]

This point of view is difficult for Americans to grasp, but crucial to traditional conceptual systems of the Far East and of other
parts of the world as well. For our purposes here, it is important to
note how thoroughly these differing conceptual patterns are integrat-

152

ed in youth cultures. Their action implications, like the action implications of radical inter-generational discontinuities, are extremely crucial. Where one's individual rights are conceived as antithetical to one's group obligations—even as irreconcilable—the person places himself conceptually in a conflict situation. But this problem is to a large extent conceptually created and conceptually avoided. Here again is evidence of the extraordinary reach and power of culturally patterned styles of thinking.

In this final chapter we have noted patterns defining the end of childhood and the nature of adolescents. From an objective point of view, however, all of childhood represents a transition, and one that the young in the United States, at least, are eager to complete (Kimball).

It is misleading to speak of "the adolescent," as psychologists and other "experts" in the United States are inclined to do. Behavior in adolescence, as in other phases of the life span, expresses the elements of a biocultural mix. No doubt there are some universal bio-elements at work; early youth is likely to be marked by high energy levels, for example. As childhood ends young people, becoming aware of impending new roles, may become restless to test themselves. However, such youth traits vary widely in accord with associated cultural elements by which they may be enhanced, contained, or otherwise affected.

In a number of cultures the child-to-adult progression is of a "gradualist" sort (Norbeck el al). It is expected that the transition ordinarily will proceed quite smoothly as the child acquires experience. But in many cultures childhood is thought of as a succession of stages, and the last of them is likely to be an occasion for ceremony. Rites performed on such occasions serve to signal to the society the neophyte's change of status, to symbolize his separation from childhood associations, perhaps to transmit practical knowledge and esoteric lore. The rites may be lengthy, harsh, and highly dramatic. Ceremonies for girls and boys always differ. If there are elaborate ceremonies for either sex they are likely to be for boys, and girls are rarely subjected to harsh or dramatic rites.

Tribal markers of the sorts usually called "puberty rites" have no precise equivalents in complex cultures. The latter instead mark the attainment of achievement levels in given activity systems—in education (by graduation) or in religion (by confirmation), for example. In the complex society these ceremonies signify that knowledge and maturity of a particular degree have been attained; they are not occasions for transmission of knowledge. They also lack the sex-role esoterica that are likely to be transmitted in the course of tribal ceremonies. In complex and class-stratified societies, middle-class and upper-class youth are likely to achieve formal maturity in multiple activity systems, while lower-class youth may experience no such ceremonial marker at all.

NOTES

[1] Solon T. Kimball, personal communication, 1967.

[2] Lois W. Hoffman and Martin L. Hoffman, eds., *Review of Child Development Research* (New York: Russell Sage Foundation, 1966), II, 491 (italics original).

[3] Edward Norbeck, Donald E. Walker, and Mimi Cohen, "The Interpretation of Data: Puberty Rites," *American Anthropologist,* 64 (1962), 463-485.

[4] E. Adamson Hoebel, *The Cheyennes* (New York: Holt, Rinehart & Winston, 1960), p. 99.

[5] Norbeck et al., "The Interpretation of Data: Puberty Rites," *op. cit.,* p. 478.

[6] *Ibid.,* p. 482.

[7] Mary Ellen Goodman, "Influences of Childhood and Adolescence," in Edward Norbeck, Douglass Price-Williams, and William M. McCord, eds., *The Study of Personality* (New York: Holt, Rinehart & Winston, 1968), p. 191.

[8] *Ibid.,* p. 190.

[9] S. N. Eisenstadt, *From Generation to Generation* (New York: The Free Press of Glencoe paperback, 1964), pp. 31 f. (paraphrased).

[10] W. E. H. Stanner, "Durmugam, a Nangiomeri," in Joseph B. Casagrande, ed., *In the Company of Man* (New York: Harper and Row, 1960), p. 95 (italics original).

[11] James B. Watson, "A New Guinea 'Opening Man'," in Casagrande, *op. cit.,* p. 144.

[12] *Ibid.,* p. 146.

[13] Sister M. Inez Hilger, *Arapaho Child Life and Its Cultural Background* (Washington, D.C.: Bureau of American Ethnology, 1952, Bulletin 148), p. 223.

[14] Napoleon A. Chagnon, *Yanomano—The Fierce People* (New York: Holt, Rinehart & Winston, 1968), p. 85.

[15] Hildred Geertz, *The Javanese Family* (New York: The Free Press of Glencoe, 1961), p. 119.

[16] E. Harwood, "Social Development in the Queensland Adolescent," *The Australian Journal of Education,* 3 (1959), 87.

[17] Chiang Yee, *A Chinese Childhood* (New York: The John Day Co., 1952), pp. 9 f.

[18] Francis L. K. Hsu, Blanche G. Watrous, and Edith M. Lord, "Culture Pattern and Adolescent Behavior," *International Journal of Social Psychiatry,* 7 (1961), 48.

[19] *Ibid.,* p. 43.

[20] *Ibid.,* p. 51.

[21] Bartlett H. Stoodley, *Society and Self* (New York: The Free Press of Glencoe, 1962), p. 208.

[22] *Ibid.*, p. 215.

Bartlett H. Stoodley, *Society and Self* (New York: The Free Press of Glencoe, 1962), p. 203.

Ibid., p. 215.

Conclusion

Cross-cultural studies and comparisons can shatter facile generalizations about children, about what "the child" perceives, knows, and feels, from infancy to adolescence. That much must be clear in light of even such limited cross-cultural documentation as this small book allows. It must be clear also that facile generalizations, cross-culturally untested, are all too numerous among the assumptions on which American parents and educators act in their dealings with the young. This is much more than merely an academic issue; it is a fact that underlies much unsound child rearing and unsound pedagogy.

If we are to improve significantly both the child rearing and the pedagogy we must begin by eliminating misconceptions about the culture of childhood. We must stop assuming that what we see, or think we see, in the children of our society at this time necessarily tells us what is universal or inevitable. Each supposed "universal" must be subjected to the cross-cultural test. It fails the test if it does not hold true in even one society. And if it is not a universal it is not inevitable; the behavior in question can be changed.

In fact there appear to be remarkably few universals, few exceptionless "laws" of childhood and its culture. The anthropological record speaks eloquently on this point, and makes clear that an enormous range of variation exists and is tolerable. This is not to say that the cultural arrangements affecting children in different societies are necessarily of equal quality of appropriateness. It is to say, however, that children can and do tolerate and even thrive under conditions our society labels cruel or psychologically destructive.

In traditional Greek villages parents and other family members will deliberately and viciously tease, frighten, and lie to little children. The elders have their reasons; they are preparing the children for the kind of social world in which they will live.[1] The important point is that this treatment does not produce a generation of psychotics, or even of neurotics, as popular assumptions in the United States might lead one to predict. The village children acquire what is essential in the childhood culture of their world—a highly developed ability to identify taunts, challenges, and lies, and to respond with enthusiasm, while preserving a degree of "cool" American teenagers might envy. For Greek adults the pattern has to do with honor and shame; it is sometimes of life-and-death importance. For the children it is a game one learns early how to play, and it lends excitement and drama to the generally quiet round of village life.

This Greek pattern illustrates universals as well as a culturally specific feature. The children learn early not only the rules of the game and how to play it. They learn also that the elders who introduce them to the pattern mean them no harm. The teacher conveys this lesson by a display of affection that follows his teasing, frightening, or lying to the child. Resentment and hostility are not generated. It *is* a "law" that children have great need for affection and a conviction that there are older and wiser people on whom they can depend for care and guidance. But we grossly underestimate their sensibilities if we assume that children are unable to identify affection and guidance, however bizarre (from our point of view) its cultural packaging. They can and do.

Parents and teachers ought to find the lessons from the cross-cultural record not only instructive but also emancipating. Much of the anxiety that seems so prevalent among them is quite unnecessary. The modes of successful child rearing and pedagogy are many, and so are the goals. A few universals must be observed. Beyond that the selection of a mode depends on one's goals.

Of the few universals, affection and guidance head the list. If broadly interpreted they, in fact, constitute the whole list. Children need repeated and consistent demonstrations of affection and guidance, and the latter no less than the former. Every attention, however mundane, can convey the message that affection is felt by the older, attending person. Every act of guidance, including severe disciplinary measures, can convey the message of affectionate concern. But guidance is essential in its own right. The word is used here to cover training and teaching, such that the child is equipped with knowledge and standards needed for successful living in his society.

In "primitive" societies life is relatively simple for everyone, parents and other socializers included. It is also harder, shorter, and more perilous, of course. But elders in such societies, at least, enjoy a large measure of freedom from anxiety about what lessons to teach and how to teach them. The traditional patterns, thoroughly

158

inculcated generation after generation, answer most of the questions. By the same token they largely remove opportunities for innovation and for individualistic choices. Every social arrangement has its own price.

We may or may not envy "primitives"; in modern urban societies we have no choice but to face the complexities and ambiguities inevitable in the culture of such societies. However, it is not necessary to agonize over child rearing and pedagogy as many of us do. The essentials—the universals—remain. It is our responsibility to provide sustained affection and guidance, just as "primitives" must. Also, we have to decide on goals—on the kind of society we want our children equipped to live in and to strengthen. These decisions have little to do with changing technology, and much to do with ideals and values.

In this matter of ideals and values there are crucial lessons to be learned from the cross-cultural record. The most obvious is the lesson that there is no necessary correlation between "primitiveness" in material conditions of living and the nature of culturally patterned ideals and values. The Bushmen of the South African Kalihari desert barely survive in a harsh environment with a minimal tool kit and the simplest set of patterns affecting food-getting, shelter, and other "necessities" of life. But they are a kindly, gentle, sharing people who abhor selfishness and cruelty.[2] Their ideals for human conduct will stand comparison with those of the most "humane" societies, and far exceed in humaneness the ideals of many a complex society. Technological complexity is no guarantee of comparable advance in standards of human conduct, but neither is such advance ruled out by technological complexity.

The society of the United States prides itself on its ideals and values, regarding them as representing something of a high in the history of human societies. Whether or not the self-congratulation is entirely justified, the fact remains that our cultural traditions in this department are indeed strong and conducive to decency in human relations. But we have yet to set our sights firmly on these traditions as major goals in child rearing and pedagogy. In our practices, it has been the means rather than the goals of rearing and teaching on which our attention has been focused. The firm inculcation of ideals and values as a goal appears to have receded into the background of our attention. The cross-cultural record shows clearly that adults, however unsophisticated about means, can be highly successful in teaching what they regard as unquestionable goals. So can we.

We can teach what we believe in. But certain diverting and unsound assumptions must be laid aside. It is unsound to assume that

159

the peer group must necessarily exercise more influence than adults. To believe that it must is to invite peer-group tyranny and to bow to it before it comes, as it will if it is expected.

It is unsound to assume that intergenerational conflict is a universal. It is not, though neither is an identity of viewpoints and interests between the generations to be expected. But the differences can be bridged, with mutual affection and restraint. They will not be bridged if on both sides there is a conviction that conflict is inevitable.

It is unsound to assume that an orderly society can be maintained by people who value neither order nor the security and dignity of others. Disorder and callous indifference to the rights and feelings of others become inevitable when little children are held to be incapable of "understanding" the needs of other people, and of respecting those needs. If they are not held accountable, from infancy, for the effects of their acts on others, then willful and egocentric children will become lawless and callous adults.

It is unsound to assume that an orderly society can be maintained without duly constituted authorities and respect for the rules and laws they must enforce. There will be disorder and defiance in a society whose children are expected and allowed to defy authority and to set themselves above it as judges of its prerogatives and their own behavior.

It is unsound to assume that an orderly society can be maintained by citizens whose concern for their rights overshadows and outweighs their willingness to assume responsibilities. There will be persistent clamor for increased rights, and indifference to responsibilities, in a society whose children are nearly always given precedence over their elders. They will grow up convinced that their claims should take first place always, and they will fail even to conceive of reciprocal responsibilities.

These are lessons from the cross-cultural record. They are unequivocal, they square with "folk wisdom" and with the "intuitions" of wise teachers and parents in modern, complex societies. It is my hope that the cross-cultural lessons illustrated in this book may serve to hearten and strengthen parents and teachers as they go about that greatest and most challenging of vocations—the affectionate guidance of the oncoming generation.

NOTES

[1] Ernestine Friedl, *Vasilika: A Village in Modern Greece* (New York: Holt, Rinehart & Winston, 1962), pp. 78 f.

[2] Elizabeth Marshall Thomas, *The Harmless People* (New York: Alfred A. Knopf, 1959).

Index